Leading Issues in Business Research Methods
Volume 2

Edited by

Dr John Mendy
Dr. Susan D. Geringer

Leading Issues in Business Research Methods: Volume Two

Disclaimer: While every effort has been made by the editor, authors and
the publishers to ensure that all the material in this book is accurate and
correct at the time of going to press, any error made by readers as a result
of any of the material, formulae or other information in this book is the
sole responsibility of the reader. Readers should be aware that the URLs
quoted in the book may change or be damaged by malware between the
time of publishing and accessing by readers.

Note to readers: Some papers have been written by authors who use the
American form of spelling and some use the British. These two different
approaches have been left unchanged.

ISBN: 978-1-910810-37-8 (print)
         978-1-910810-38-5 (e-Pub)
         978-1-910810-39-2 (Kindle)

Printed by Lightning Source POD

Published by: Academic Conferences and Publishing International Limited,
Reading, RG4 9AY, United Kingdom, info@academic-publishing.org
Available from www.academic-bookshop.com

Contents

About the editors

Susan Geringer, (DBA, MA, BA) is an Associate Professor in the Department of Marketing & Logistics at California State University, Fresno. Susan completed her BA and MA degrees at California State University, Sacramento, conducted post-graduate work at New York University and received her DBA from Henley Business School, University of Reading. She has a number of research interests, including Consumer Behavior, Marketing Education, Sports Marketing, Fashion Marketing, Marketing Research and Business Research Methodology. Susan is a member of the Executive Board of the Marketing Management Association and serves as a reviewer for a number of marketing journals. In addition, she actively publishes in a number of academic research journals.

John Mendy, (PhD, MCIPD, FHEA) John has spent the better part of his life researching, teaching and learning. He has taught a range of Business and Management modules and is currently MSc HRM Programme Leader, University of Lincoln. John has published and continues to review for a range of national and international refereed journals and other publication outlets. His research interests include Research on research, Complexity, HRM and Organisational Behaviour, Organisational becoming and improvement, organisational culture and change, change management, individual and collective preferences, values and attitudes.

List of Contributing Authors

Edwin Asiamah Acheampong, *University of Bolton, UK*
Greg Baatard, *Edith Cowan University, Perth, Australia*
Graeme Baxter, *Robert Gordon University, Aberdeen, UK*
Frank Bezzina, *Department of Management, Faculty of Economics, Management and Accountancy, University of Malta, Msida*
Karl Joachim Breunig, *School of Business, Oslo and Akershus University College, Norway*
Line Christoffersen, *School of Business, Oslo and Akershus University College, Norway*
Elena Fitkov-Norris, *Kingston University, London, UK*
Faridah Hj Hassan, *Universiti Teknologi MARA, Shah Alam, Malaysia*
Nurlida Ismail, *Taylor's University, Subang Jaya, Malaysia*
Kondal Reddy Kondadi, *University of Bolton, UK*
Becky Lees, *Kingston University, London, UK*
Rita Marcella, *Robert Gordon University, Aberdeen, UK*
Ellen Martins, *Organisational Diagnostics, Johannesburg, South Africa*
Nico Martins, *Department of Industrial and Organisational Psychology, College of Economic Sciences, Unisa, Pretoria, South Africa*
John Mendy, *University of Lincoln, UK*
Marcia Mkansi, *University of Bolton, UK*
Baomin Qi, *University of Bolton, UK*
Hayley Rowlands, *Robert Gordon University, Aberdeen, UK*
Mark Saunders, *Surrey Business School, Faculty of Business, Economics and Law, University of Surrey, UK*
Nooraini Mohamad Sheriff, *Universiti Teknologi MARA, Shah Alam, Malaysia*
Wallace Yee, *Faculty of Business Administration, University of Macau, China*
Ruth Yeung, *Institute for Tourism Studies, Macao, China*

Introduction to Leading Issues in Business and Management Research, Volume 2

Since it started publishing academic research and project-type papers in 2002, the Electronic Journal of Business Research Methods (EJBRM) has covered enormous ground on research perspectives, processes and issues. Through its publications, the journal has sought to continuously and constantly shed light on Business and Management issues and it is anticipated that the current second volume of Leading Issues in Business Management Research will build on from the first volume and add to the contributions of EJBRM. A wide array of topics in this growing area of research range from consumer, employer and employee behaviour to Business Research models, methods and methodologies, systems and processes and the use of web-based techniques and technologies. It is anticipated this second volume will continue to give a platform for academics and practitioners in their respective fields to showcase as wide a range of research interests and aspirations as is available.

In selecting the current papers, the editors have sought to cover a representative set of papers from both quantitative and qualitative strands. Papers that set out what research methods were adopted, their epistemological and philosophical positions, considerations of alternative research methods (interviews, surveys, the Web, focus groups...) and epistemological positions (positivism, interpretivism, constructivism...), why these might not have been chosen and what contributions were made to the field have generally been selected for the current volume. It is the editors' view that established and early career researchers as well as students learning to do research will benefit from the selection.

Likewise papers that clearly identified their research question(s) or research focus and were guided throughout by the related research issues gained recognition. The editors also gave due considerations to papers that problematized issues such as where data was going to be obtained, the nature and quality of the data, how the latter was going to be analysed and the impact of the research process on research quality, reliability, validity and in some instances, generalizability.

Papers in this volume generally show a good range of research methods, some of which do not necessarily fall within the traditional types of methods that one would normally read about in the research methods textbooks and guides in terms of their implementation. Papers that also looked at the growing number of research issues involved in ICT/web-based research, organisational access and data collection, their presentation and analyses as well as those that reported the findings from an ongoing project also gained recognition in the current volume. The selection was also swayed to papers that opened up new strands of research thinking, research dissemination and methodological implementation as well as the potential difficulties in the choices of one's selected research methods, techniques and their implementation. The debate on open-access dissemination of research is an area in which the ECRM and EJBRM are championing amongst other things and one that would, it seems from emerging research, continue for some time.

The current selection totals ten papers which highlight a variety of research questions, problems and issues and an accompanying range of research methods and methodological discussions. Their authors have stated the research positions they have adopted and respectable levels of justification and knowledge forms have been presented. These range from those forms of knowledge that might be found of practical usage to those that are more academically inclined. A certain level of research impact is either implied or overtly presented in the selected papers.

Dr John Mendy
University of Lincoln
Lincoln Business School
jmendy@lincoln.ac.uk

Dr. Susan D. Geringer
California State University, Fresno
Craig School of Business
sgeringer@csufresno.edu

A Technical Guide to Designing and Implementing Effective Web Surveys

Greg Baatard
Edith Cowan University, Perth, Australia
Originally published in ECRM (2012) Conference Proceedings

Editorial Commentary

The paper tackles the important, emerging phenomenon of the use of the internet/web to conduct data collection for a growing number of studies. Despite the growing interest in the area, a number of issues need attention such as how to design, deliver and administer web surveys as well as how to structure, present and layout of the questions asked. The paper explores some of the decisions in these areas and how they can impact on how efficient and effective the designed survey is for its users and what is intended. Recommendations are drawn and the resulting issue of data quality explored in line with attempts to enhance the effectiveness of the research process.

Abstract: The Internet is becoming an increasingly prominent medium for the administration of surveys. Although individual findings vary, the majority of the literature agrees that the appropriateness and response rates of web surveys is expected to rise in the future as we enter a generation of "digital natives" and mail-based communication becomes increasingly antiquated. Just about every aspect and tenet of traditional survey methodology has received attention in academic literature, positioning it as one of the most mature data collection techniques and a mainstay in all areas of research. While much of this accumulated knowledge is applicable and relevant to web surveys, there are numerous issues that arise specifically when surveys are delivered online. Such issues concern the overall design, delivery and administration of web surveys and the structure, presentation and layout of their questions. The decisions made in these areas can influence the efficacy of a web survey in a number of ways, including the rate, integrity and quality of responses. This paper discusses such issues, and makes a number of recommen-

1

dations to assist researchers in manually developing an effective web survey and in evaluating survey creation products and services.

Keywords: web, online, survey, questionnaire, guide

1 Introduction

Dillman, Smyth and Christian (2009) describe the past two decades as "turbulent times" for the survey methodology. The telephone-based surveys popular throughout the 1970s and 1980s have become substantially less popular amongst researchers, marred by numerous factors including a surge in telemarketing and the distasteful phenomenon of receiving calls during the "dinner hour". While still heavily used and indeed the most suitable medium in some demographics, mail-based surveys have begun to lose ground with advances in technology spurring web surveys to prominence. As Internet access and eMail become almost synonymous with the ownership of or access to a personal computer, delivering self-administered surveys via such technologies has become an increasingly common practice. Doing so offers the same benefits of mail surveys – allowing the researcher to reach potential respondents all over the world with minimal cost of data collection and processing. Furthermore, web surveys require less effort by respondents to complete and return than mail surveys (Couper 2000; Fricker and Schonlau 2002; Lyons, Cude et al. 2005; Deutskens, de Ruyter et al. 2006; Couper and Miller 2008; Malhotra 2008; Dillman, Smyth et al. 2009; Vicente and Reis 2010). The medium also affords greater control in terms of validation and the delivery of the survey items; for example, conditional questions can be presented only if required (Oppenheim 1992; Couper 2000; Fricker and Schonlau 2002; Shropshire, Hawdon et al. 2009; Vicente and Reis 2010).

The already low response rates typically seen in mail surveys are set to become lower still as more and more communication occurs electronically, making the completion and return of a printed survey a somewhat archaic process. Dillman, et al. (2009) echo this sentiment, stating that "the shift toward eMail as the communication mode of choice for significant sectors of the population is somewhat ironic as it is one of the very factors that make Internet surveys possible, but it is also making surveys by traditional modes more difficult to complete." Web surveys normally require no more than eMail and/or a Web browser to complete and submit – both of which the large majority of today's computer users are familiar with. Furthermore, the completion of trivial online quizzes, polls and tests has emerged as a social pastime for many Internet users, particularly those in teen and young adult demographics (Fricker and Schonlau 2002). Although done for amusement, these activities serve to familiarise Internet users with the mechanics of web surveys and potentially increase their willingness to respond to other surveys.

Several studies conducted in the past decade have found that web surveys can achieve similar response rates to mail surveys, particularly for younger respondents and those in demographics that regularly use the Internet. Some of the studies finding response rates to mail surveys to be higher than those of web surveys have also acknowledged the need to take demographics into account and the likelihood of response rates differing in the future. These trends suggest that web surveys will become increasingly prominent and result in higher response rates as the population becomes increasingly made up of "digital natives" (Jones and Pitt 1999; Cook, Heath et al. 2000; Couper 2000; Couper, Traugott et al. 2001; Fricker and Schonlau 2002; Kaplowitz, Hadlock et al. 2004; van Selm and Jankowski 2006; Lusk, Delclos et al. 2007; Converse, Wolfe et al. 2008; Couper and Miller 2008; Shih and Fan 2008). Indeed, the emergence of the Internet as a major medium for the delivery of self-administered surveys is easily observable and cannot be denied.

The issues of survey design are well established and mature in academic literature, covering topics such as question wording, question types and survey length. While such issues are entirely applicable and must be respected in web surveys, this paper focuses upon issues which arise specifically when surveys are delivered online. The issues discussed can have a significant impact upon the accessibility and usability of web surveys, potentially influencing both response rates and the quality of responses themselves – "Before writing a questionnaire for the web, it is important to remember that a poorly designed survey can discourage people from responding, and it can also give skewed results" (Gonzalez-Bañales and Adam 2007). Several of the issues and recommendations are of a technical nature, written with the assumption that interested readers will have a moderate level of technical knowledge or at least an understanding of the technical aspects of developing and implementing a web survey.

2 Overall design, delivery and administration issues

This section discusses the primary issues related to the overall design, delivery and administration of web surveys as a whole. The first issue is that of the delivery and hosting of the survey. The author recommends against utilising eMail for anything other than contacting potential respondents, despite possibly appearing as a method of minimising the effort required to respond. While it is possible to embed or attach a survey to an eMail, this practice is relatively uncommon and is less likely to be supported in a uniform fashion by eMail client software (Fricker and Schonlau 2002; Lyons, Cude et al. 2005). Thus, response rates of eMail-based surveys may be hampered by both unfamiliarity and technical hurdles. Web surveys should be hosted on the Internet as standard Web pages. They should minimise any reliance on supporting software or technologies such as Flash or JavaScript (Kaczmirek 2005; Gonzalez-Bañales and Adam 2007). As discussed in the next section, if such technologies are used they should not be relied upon and the survey should function properly without their presence. Like all Web pages, all web surveys should be tested thoroughly before deployment to ensure that they appear and function correctly in all likely browsers, browser versions, screen resolutions, and so forth (Fricker and Schonlau 2002; Thompson, Surface et al. 2003; Kaczmirek 2005; Lyons, Cude et al. 2005; Gonzalez-Bañales and Adam 2007).

Access to and availability of web surveys must also be considered. In addition to adhering to appropriate sampling procedures (Simsek and Veiga 2001; Lyons, Cude et al. 2005; van Selm and Jankowski 2006; Couper and Miller 2008; Vicente and Reis 2010), web surveys should require some form of unique identifier such as an ID number, code, IP address or eMail address to deter automated responses or multiple responses by a single person (Couper, Traugott et al. 2001; Thompson, Surface et al. 2003; Lyons, Cude et al. 2005). Such measures can increase the quality of the data gathered by deterring behaviour which negatively influences response data. When using an ID number or access code, Couper, et al. (2001) recommend avoiding those containing potentially ambiguous characters such as the letter "l" and the number "1" or the letter "o" and the number "0". Limiting the availability of a web survey has the potential to strengthen the data set. For example, if a survey is to be administered only to employees of a single organisation, it may be appropriate to deploy it in such a way that it can only be accessed via the organisation's internal network (Simsek and Veiga 2001). Controlling and limiting the availability of a web survey also serve to prevent abuse. Though the likelihood of this is minimal for most surveys, this is of particular importance if the survey concerns topics considered to be controversial, sensitive or high-profile. The potential for abuse has been illustrated several times by the abuse of online polls – a different but definitely similar scenario. Time magazine's 2009 "Time 100" poll was manipulated with enough sophistication to arrange the top 21 results (Schonfeld 2009). A similar hoax in 2010 targeted singer Justin Beiber; an online poll being abused in order to add North Korea as a desti-nation in his first world tour (Emery 2010).

It is worthwhile at this point to acknowledge that numerous applications and Web-based services exist, which can be used to create and administer web surveys. Modern products offer high degrees of customisability and sophistication, allowing a web survey to be created and administered with minimal technical knowledge. While reviews or recommendations of these are not included in this paper (interested readers see for example, Thompson, Surface et al. 2003; Wright 2005 and http://websm.org/), the issues discussed here can serve as criteria by which to assess such applica-tions or services. In addition, one must consider factors such as the cost and the confidentiality, security and ownership of data when determining their suitability (Lyons, Cude et al. 2005; Wright 2005; Greenlaw and Brown-Welty 2009). Despite the availability of these products, various fac-tors often make a purpose-built web survey a necessity.

A final consideration pertinent to the overall design of web surveys is that of the processing and storage of responses. The ability to store response data directly in a database or spreadsheet format is a definite advantage of administering surveys electronically, and this can be maximised with a well-designed web survey (Lyons, Cude et al. 2005; Gonzalez-Bañales and Adam 2007; Greenlaw and Brown-Welty 2009). A web survey is essentially a form, and as such must be processed like any other Web-based form once submitted. Although it is possible to create a form which simply eMails the response to the researcher, entering the response into a data-base is a much more effective method. This can be facilitated by ensuring that the names of the form elements such as text fields and radio button groups correspond to the database column names, allowing simple and generic form processing scripts to be created. Care should be taken to en-sure that web surveys are submitted and stored in a secure manner, utilis-ing appropriate encryption (Lyons, Cude et al. 2005). As well as being easily exportable to spreadsheet or statistical analysis software formats, survey responses in a database can be queried using SQL (Structured Query Language), offering sophisticated means of extracting and visualising meaningful information. To allow effective querying, the values submitted in a web survey should be numeric wherever appropriate. For example, a five-point Likert scale question ranging from Strongly Disagree to Strongly Agree and including a Neutral response should be stored as -2 to 2 with 0 representing Neutral, rather than storing responses textually.

This section has mainly discussed issues that aim to improve the quality, correctness, usability and reliability of data gathered via web surveys. The recommendations are overarching – benefiting the researcher directly, rather than via the improvement of the respondent's experience. The following sections focus upon issues that improve the respondent's experience.

3   Structure, presentation and question layout issues

This section discusses issues of structure, presentation and question layout within web surveys that can influence the respondent's experience. Regardless of the medium, a survey that is clear, convenient and usable is of more appeal to potential respondents, resulting in higher response rates and potentially better quality data. The author feels it is important to make all relevant information available with the survey itself. While eMail or other methods may be used to introduce the research and request participation, all pertinent information should also be available with the web survey. While this may result in some redundancy, it ensures that respondents do not need to search outside of the survey Web page for any instructions or information they may need. While minor, inconveniences such as these have the potential to deter a respondent – particularly if they encounter the inconvenience before beginning the survey, when they have not yet invested any time or effort into its completion.

The issue of survey length has been addressed in numerous pieces of academic literature, often finding that longer surveys are not only less likely to be completed, but also that "questions asked later in the questionnaire bear the risk of producing lower quality data, especially if they are in open format or in long grids" (Galesic and Bosnjak 2009). Based on such findings (Herzog and Bachman 1981; Gonzalez-Bañales and Adam 2007), two recommendations that are applicable to surveys in any medium are worth repeating. Lengthy surveys should be avoided if possible, and the ordering of questions should be considered in longer surveys – acknowledging that the quality of responses to questions towards the end may be lower than that of those near the beginning (Vicente and Reis 2010). A further consideration regarding the ordering of questions arises from Shropshire, Hawdon and Witte (2009), which found respondent interest to be a significant factor in early termination of a questionnaire. Hence, questions likely to be of highest interest to respondents should appear early in the survey. Two further recommendations can be made for lengthy web surveys in particular. Firstly, the design and presentation of the survey can be tailored to make a long survey more manageable for respondents. One method is to divide the survey into sections and display one section at a time (Figure 1).

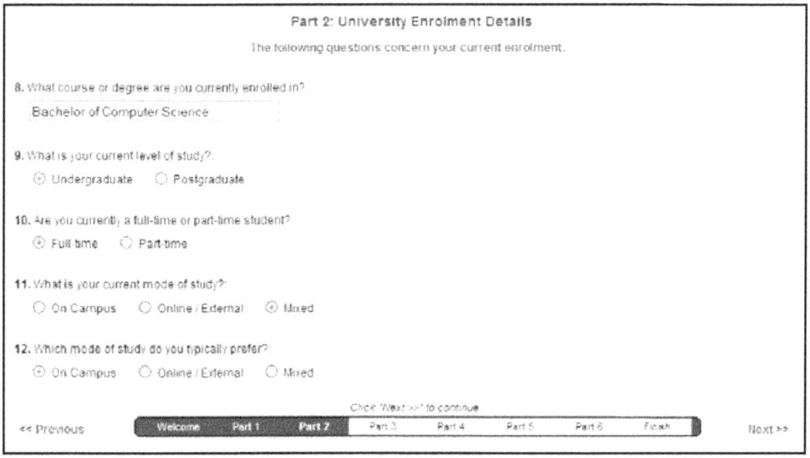

Figure 1: Example of a long survey divided into sections

This serves to avoid overwhelming the respondent with a large number of questions on one page and the need to scroll, which have been found to influence item non-response and survey non-completion rates (Couper, Traugott et al. 2001; Schonlau, Fricker et al. 2002; Toepoel, Das et al. 2008; Vicente and Reis 2010). Research (see for example, Tourangeau, Couper et al. 2004; Dillman, Smyth et al. 2009; Toepoel, Das et al. 2009) has found that respondents see questions on the same page as being more closely related, having a slight impact upon the intercorrelation of responses. This should be taken into account when determine if and how to divide a survey into multiple pages. An overall progress bar and section-by-section validation are advisable if a survey is divided into sections. Yan, Conrad, Tourangeau and Couper (2010) examine the use of a progress indicator in web surveys, concluding that it encourages completion if it accurately reflects the expected duration of the survey, particularly if the survey is short. This further emphasises the need to minimise the length of web surveys and to provide information such as its expected duration. Other research regarding the use of progress indicators in surveys divided into sections is generally supportive, however findings vary and the effects of progress indicators are often minor (Couper, Traugott et al. 2001; Crawford, Couper et al. 2001; Vicente and Reis 2010).

The second recommendation specific to lengthy web surveys is giving respondents the ability to save their progress and resume the survey at a later time. This is recommended in Kaczmirek (2005), who states "Do not introduce problems in your online questionnaire which would not occur in a paper and pencil questionnaire." While implementing the ability to save and resume survey progress is likely to be beyond the technical capabilities of a person otherwise capable of creating a web survey, the feature is common amongst applications and Web-based services that allow surveys to be created.

Unlike mail surveys, web surveys can adapt to a respondent's answers to questions on the fly. In a mail survey, conditional questions are typically implemented via instructions to the respondent – for example, "If you answered 'No' to this question, continue to Question 12". Using Web-based scripting languages such as JavaScript, web surveys can implement conditional questions in a more effective manner, showing or hiding parts of the survey based on the answers to questions (Oppenheim 1992; Fricker and Schonlau 2002; Gonzalez-Bañales and Adam 2007). In addition to helping to ensure the correctness of data, this serves to "reduce the length of a survey to the individual minimum" (Kaczmirek 2005). Though JavaScript can improve the implementation of web surveys, it is inadvisable to rely upon it heavily. Ideally it should be possible and convenient to complete the survey without requiring the respondent's browser to have JavaScript enabled. If the survey cannot be completed without JavaScript, potential respondents with JavaScript disabled should be informed of its need when they attempt to access it.

The following recommendations concern the presentation, layout, accessibility and formatting of web survey questions. While some of the recommendations are relatively minor, they are all worthy of consideration when creating a web survey or deciding which survey-generation product to use. Research such as that of Christian, Dillman and Smyth (2007) underpin the potential effects of seemingly minor issues in web survey presentation, finding that the relative size of text fields resulted in an eight percent increase in correctly formatted responses and the use of symbols rather than words as labels resulted in a seven percent increase. In order to avoid excess technical detail, the recommendations are presented in dot-point form. The term "form elements" refers to text fields, radio buttons, checkboxes and other form components used to allow people to respond to questions in web surveys.

- Make use of space to clearly separate questions from one another. If utilising a grid-based layout, often used to present series of Likert scale questions, use alternating background colours to clearly align question text with the appropriate form elements.
- Use spacing to ensure that radio buttons and checkboxes are clearly associated with their labels, preventing ambiguity and confusion. Furthermore, use the "label" tag to increase the clickable region of form elements. These points are illustrated in Figure 2.

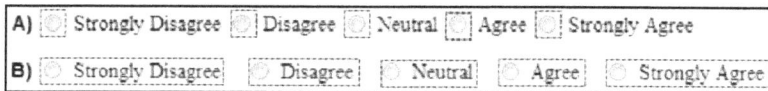

Figure 2: Likert scale with ambiguous spacing and no labels (A) and Likert scale with clear spacing and labels (B). Clickable regions have been highlighted

- If there is insufficient space to repeat labels next to each radio button or checkbox, consider using the "title" attribute in the "<input>" or "<label>" tag. The content of this attribute will appear as a tooltip when the mouse is over the radio button, allowing respondents to select a response without needing to refer back to other labels.
- The layout of Likert scale responses is explored in Tourangeau, Couper and Conrad (2004), who find that respondents make inferences about the meaning of survey items based on visual cues such as the perceived midpoint of responses, their spacing and

order. These findings should be taken into consideration when designing Likert scales in web surveys.

- If a question requires participants to select from a number of options, use radio buttons rather than drop down lists as radio buttons present the options in a more convenient and accessible manner. Healey (2007) found that drop-down lists result in higher item non-response rates, longer response times and increased accidental changing of responses. Kaczmirek (2005) recommends only using drop-down lists "if respondents know the answer without having to look at all entries", and to make the default selection is a placeholder such as "select here" so that non-response can be identified.

- Users can navigate form elements via the tab key, with each press bringing the focus to the next element from top-left to bottom-right. The layout of form elements in a survey may cause the default tab order to traverse form elements in an incorrect or unintuitive manner. If this is the case, the ordering can be changed via the "tabindex" in form element tags. The "accesskey" attribute can also be used to allow keyboard shortcuts to form elements if deemed necessary for accessibility reasons.

- On the spot validation of responses is possible in web surveys, via scripting languages such as JavaScript. While it is possible to enforce strict validation criteria such as only allowing digits to appear in a text field for a phone number, it is not always advisable to do so. When faced with overly strict, inappropriate or frustrating validation requirements, respondents may invent data, attempt to circumvent the validation, or discontinue the survey entirely (Best and Krueger 2004; Kaczmirek 2005; Christian, Dillman et al. 2007; Gonzalez-Bañales and Adam 2007; Vicente and Reis 2010). It is also worthwhile reiterating that reliance upon JavaScript is not recommended.

Failing to take heed of issues such as these can lead to web surveys which are unclear, confusing and frustrating, often resulting in discontinuation or by respondent, or lower quality data. By taking these recommendations into consideration, researchers can design, develop and implement an effective web survey, or select a product which will allow them to create one.

4 Conclusion

There is much academic literature which addresses the design and implementation of effective surveys. Of that, a relatively small proportion discusses issues specific to the increasingly prominent medium of Internet-based surveys. Web surveys present unique opportunities and challenges not applicable to mail-based surveys, and care must be taken to ensure that web surveys are developed and implemented in an effective manner. This paper has discussed numerous issues, primarily technical, that should be taken into consideration in regards to web surveys.

Issues pertaining to the overall design, delivery and administration of web surveys were covered first. EMail-based surveys are advised against, and the importance of appropriate advertising, unique identifiers and data format were discussed. The recommendations in this section seek to give researchers overarching guidance towards creating web surveys that are more likely to produce data of high quality, correctness, usability and reliability. Next, a number of recommendations were made regarding the structure, presentation and layout of questions in web surveys. These focus upon increasing the clarity, convenience and usability of web surveys, promoting higher response rates and higher quality data.

As the world's population becomes increasingly made up of "digital natives", the Internet has emerged as a key medium for self-administered surveys. The sophistication and availability of modern applications and Web-based services for the creation of web surveys has also made the medium more accessible to researchers in all domains, furthering their use. The recommendations made in this paper assist researchers both in manually developing a web survey and evaluating survey creation products. A well-developed web survey provides both the researcher and respondents with a clear, accessible and highly usable mechanism, minimising the confusing and frustrating elements that may lower response rates or the quality of data.

References

Best, S. J., and Krueger, B. (2004). Internet Data Collection. Thousand Oaks, CA, SAGE Publications.

Christian, L. M., Dillman, D. A., and Smyth, J. D. (2007). "Helping Respondents Get It Right the First Time: The Influence of Words, Symbols, and Graphics in Web Surveys" Public Opinion Quarterly, Vol 71, No. 1, pp 113-125.

Converse, P. D., Wolfe, E. W., Huang, X., and Oswald, F. L. (2008). "Response Rates for Mixed-Mode Surveys Using Mail and EMail/Web." American Journal of Evaluation, Vol 29, No. 1, pp 99-107.

Cook, C., Heath, F., and Thompson, R. L. (2000). "A Meta-Analysis of Response Rates in Web- or Internet-Based Surveys." Educational and Psychological Measurement, Vol 60, No. 6, pp 821-836.

Couper, M. P. (2000). "Web surveys: A review of issues and approaches." Public Opinion Quarterly, Vol 64, No. 4, pp 464-494.

Couper, M. P., and Miller, P. V. (2008). "Web Survey Methods: Introduction." Public Opinion Quarterly, Vol 72, No. 5, pp 831-835.

Couper, M. P., Traugott, M. W., and Lamias, M. J. (2001). "Web Survey Design and Administration." Public Opinion Quarterly, Vol 65, No. 2, pp 230-253.

Crawford, S. D., Couper, M. P., and Lamias, M. J. (2001). "Web surveys: Perception of burden." Social Science Computer Review, Vol 19, No. 2, pp 146-162.

Deutskens, E., de Ruyter, K., and Wetzels, M. (2006). "An Assessment of Equivalence Between Online and Mail Surveys in Service Research." Journal of Service Research, Vol 8, No. 4, pp 346-355.

Dillman, D. A., Smyth, J. D., and Christian, L. M. (2009). Internet, Mail, and Mixed-Mode Surveys: The Tailored Design Method. Hoboken, New Jersey, John Wiley & Sons, Inc.

Emery, D. (2010). "Prank leaves Justin Bieber facing tour of North Korea." BBC News Retrieved 15/12/11, from http://www.bbc.co.uk/news/10506482.

Fricker, R. D., and Schonlau, M. (2002). "Advantages and Disadvantages of Internet Research Surveys: Evidence from the Literature." Field Methods, Vol 14, No. 4, pp 347-367.

Galesic, M., and Bosnjak, M. (2009). "Effects of Questionnaire Length on Participation and Indicators of Response Quality in a Web Survey." Public Opinion Quarterly, Vol 73, No. 2, pp 349-360.

Gonzalez-Bañales, D. L., and Adam, M. R. (2007). Web Survey Design and Implementation: Best Practices for Empirical Research. European and Mediterranean Conference on Information Systems, Valencia, Spain.

Greenlaw, C., and Brown-Welty, S. (2009). "A Comparison of Web-Based and Paper-Based Survey Methods: Testing Assumptions of Survey Mode and Response Cost." Evaluation Review, Vol 33, No. 5, pp 464-480.

Healey, B. (2007). "Drop Downs and Scroll Mice: The Effect of Response Option Format and Input Mechanism Employed on Data Quality in Web Surveys." Social Science Computer Review, Vol 25, No. 1, pp 111-128.

Herzog, A. R., and Bachman, J. G. (1981). "Effects of Questionnaire Length on Response Quality." Public Opinion Quarterly, Vol 45, No. 4, pp 549-559.

Jones, R., and Pitt, N. (1999). "Health surveys in the workplace: comparison of postal, email and World Wide Web methods." Occupational Medicine, Vol 49, No. 8, pp 556-558.

Kaczmirek, L. (2005). Web Surveys. A Brief Guide on Usability and Implementation Issues. Usability Professionals 2005. M. Hassenzahl and M. Peissner. Stuttgart, Usability Professionals' Association (German Chapter): 102-105.

Kaplowitz, M. D., Hadlock, T. D., and Levine, R. (2004). "A Comparison of Web and Mail Survey Response Rates." Public Opinion Quarterly, Vol 68, No. 1, pp 94-101.

Lusk, C., Delclos, G. L., Burau, K., Drawhorn, D. D., and Aday, L. A. (2007). "Mail versus Internet surveys: Determinants of method of response preferences among health professionals." Evaluation & the Health Professions, Vol 30, No. 2, pp 186-201.

Lyons, A. C., Cude, B., Lawrence, F. C., and Gutter, M. (2005). "Conducting Research Online: Challenges Facing Researchers in Family and Consumer Sciences." Family and Consumer Sciences Research Journal, Vol 33, No. 4, pp 341-356.

Malhotra, N. (2008). "Completion Time and Response Order Effects in Web Surveys." Public Opinion Quarterly, Vol 72, No. 5, pp 914-934.

Oppenheim, A. N. (1992). Questionnaire design, interviewing, and attitude measurement. New York, Pinter Publishers.

Schonfeld, E. (2009). "4Chan Takes Over The Time 100." The Washington Post Retrieved 15/12/11, from http://www.washingtonpost.com/wp-dyn/content/article/2009/04/21/AR2009042101864.html.

Schonlau, M., Fricker, R. D., and Elliott, M. N. (2002). Conducting research surveys via eMail and the Web. Santa Monica, CA, Rand Corporation.

Shih, T.-H., and Fan, X. (2008). "Comparing Response Rates from Web and Mail Surveys: A Meta-Analysis." Field Methods, Vol 20, No. 3, pp 249-271.

Shropshire, K. O., Hawdon, J. E., and Witte, J. C. (2009). "Web Survey Design: Balancing Measurement, Response, and Topical Interest." Sociological Methods Research, Vol 37, No. 3, pp 344-370.

Simsek, Z., and Veiga, J. F. (2001). "A Primer on Internet Organizational Surveys." Organizational Research Methods, Vol 4, No. 3, pp 218-235.

Thompson, L. F., Surface, E. A., Martin, D. L., and Sanders, M. G. (2003). "From Paper to Pixels: Moving Personnel Surveys to the Web." Personnel Psychology, Vol 56, No. 1, pp 197–227.

Toepoel, V., Das, M., and van Soest, A. (2008). "Effects of Design in Web Surveys: Comparing Trained and Fresh Respondents." Public Opinion Quarterly, Vol 72, No. 5, pp 985-1007.

Toepoel, V., Das, M., and van Soest, A. (2009). "Design of Web Questionnaires: The Effects of the Number of Items per Screen " Field Methods, Vol 21, No. 2, pp 200-213.

Tourangeau, R., Couper, M. P., and Conrad, F. G. (2004). "Spacing, Position, and Order. Interpretive Heuristics for Visual Features of Survey Questions." Public Opinion Quarterly, Vol 68, No. 3, pp 368-393.

van Selm, M., and Jankowski, N. W. (2006). "Conducting Online Surveys." Quality & Quantity, Vol 40, No. 3, pp 435-456.

Vicente, P., and Reis, E. (2010). "Using Questionnaire Design to Fight Nonresponse Bias in Web Surveys." Social Science Computer Review, Vol 28, No. 2, pp 251-267.

Wright, K. B. (2005). "Researching Internet-Based Populations: Advantages and Disadvantages of Online Survey Research, Online Questionnaire Authoring Software Packages, and Web Survey Services " Journal of Computer-Mediated Communication, Vol 10, No. 3, article 11.

Yan, T., Conrad, F. G., Tourangeau, R., and Couper, M. P. (2010). "Should I Stay or Should I go: The Effects of Progress Feedback, Promised Task Duration, and Length of Questionnaire on Completing Web Surveys." International Journal of Public Opinion Research.

Searching for a Third Way: Self-Justification

John Mendy
University of Lincoln, UK
Originally published in ECRM (2012) Conference Proceedings

Editorial Commentary

The paper identifies an important research question, i.e. the ability of researchers to deal with issues related to justification. Among them are how researchers can depersonalise their findings while considering the issue of context or what the paper refers to as 'situatedness'. The paper problematizes the fact that even though justification has received much attention in research methodology literature, it is lagging behind in the area where employees in business organisations construct boundaries as a process of creating meaning from their experiences. Such experiences are framed by the tasks that employees wish to cooperate upon and potentially learn from. Such a shift in emphasising what research findings need to be justified therefore moves the debate from researchers seeking to justify their representations or even represent some given 'reality', to attempting to identify what employees in a number of organisational change situations wish to see as their justification of their personal contributions to change. In essence, the problem of justification is linked to the problem of what individual employees wish to contribute to a collective task and what they wish to learn from that. The notion of 'employees as producers' not only identifies employees' contributions to four changing organisations, but also highlights the quality of the link between individual and collective contributions and what employees learn from each other. In this instance the link between individuals and the collective is self-justified. What is missing is whether it would be possible to judge whether the resulting self-justification approach can be replicated in other organisations that may or may not be going through similar challenges that might have been the result of organisational change pressures.

Abstract: Over the years, researchers have been exploring ways of dealing with the problem of justification, partly to simplify and facilitate teaching its fundamental role and partly to improve the quality of research-in-practice. Traditionally, justification (or justifying one's research) is linked to depersonalisation, formalised in terms of criteria such as reliability and validity. The need for different forms of justification has been keenly felt due to some difficulties with this notion. The question arises: how can one depersonalise when one deals with situatedness? The arisen situation has led to a plethora of alternative criteria for justification, such as credibility, transferability, confirmability or recoverability and even usability. Each of these notions carries different interpretations according to the research purpose(s). My focus in this paper is to search for a solution of the problem of justification (or justifying) in an area where it has received insignificant attention yet: an area where people construct boundaries to their experiences by cooperating in some task. Here justification can and needs to be explored as if new. In this area justifying one's research is not aimed at sentences that traditionally seek to represent 'a' or 'the' reality. Here, people construct boundaries to their experiences by cooperating in, and thereby learning from, some task rendering the question of justification one of identifying which task boundaries are to be preferred and learnt from. The area seems to have exploded in the literature in the last decade or two. An earlier recognition of this approach was Taylorism, as part of the tradition of representing some reality. What is being treated as if new is the realisation that representation has to be replaced by something else, as follows. What people are able and wish to contribute to and learrn from, depends on what the collective task is and vice versa. If people's willingness to contribute to their development and that of the collective task is frustrated, they start to resist. In consequence, the problem of justification becomes one of linking the level of individual and that of collective experiences such that each level learns from and maintains the other even when challenged. If the latter is to happen, attempts should be made to demonstrate the link's uniqueness. This means that the process of discovery and protecting each level's learning and maintainability become justified and are combined in terms of a process of self-justification. The justification process is exemplified by the results of a study concerning the behaviour of employees in 4 organisations facing radical changes because of external challenges. It is described how certain individuals are able to take initiatives superior to their managers'. Their activity may be called 'employees as producers'. They become autonomous learners and contributors. Interestingly, they become able to link personal to collective development and thereby to contribute so their companies become more responsive to new challenges. It is argued that this means that they strive to increase the quality of the link between individual and collective contributions to each other's learning and thereby self-justify that link. This type of justification is based on the equivalence between finding a unique link between individual and global observations, similar to the case of representation. Comments are added to contextualise the problem of finding this unique link. In one it is pointed out that links between non-observational contributions are more severely restricted and more difficult to achieve than links between observational contributions, traditionally implemented using reliability and validity.

Keywords: research, justifying, coherence, procedure and learning

1 Introduction

Over the centuries, science in general and researchers in particular have been struggling to deal with the teaching and implementation of a significant problem: justification. My focus in this paper is to try to invent a procedure designed to solve this problem by talking about variety to help clarify this resurgent problem so we don't have to spend more resources in future research. The language of a production procedure is chosen, although other forms (e.g. design, approach, "superstructure" (Vahl 1997: 2)) have been used in other contexts. While some procedures have studied organisations (or the world) from the outside by using language to represent that 'world' in a depersonalised way, I intend to write about this "craving for justification" (Miller 2007: 4) from an insider's position. In the latter, the researcher is part of the situation being studied whilst there is some detachment between self and the problem one is intending to solve in 'world' in the former. In the latter, his/her actions influence what he/she produces and is influenced by participants' intentions. When one adopts the inside perspective, language becomes a structuring factor or if one wishes, research becomes (and is) a problem of what language we use to deal with a justification problem. The latter should take into account what boundaries its participants are willing to construct and thereby contribute to and to the final product/tool etc. The relation between the inside and the outside, between the researcher and his/her 'world' (as the link between structure and content of language) is mapped. Such mapping is anticipated to help us recognise what contributes to people's actions and what does not. It is further aimed at discovering where preferences lie in the individual and collective boundaries we carve out of problems and what contributes to the quality and hence the protection of the mapping. In facilitating the visibility of the linkage between these elements, we are not restricted to the predictability of outcomes or even their representation but their anticipation and situatedness. Practical procedures are provided. These should identify relevant theories and the steps taken in their structuring. The production procedure should help study respondents' statements, justify the data as used, the steps needed to collect these and what approach(es) may be developed as (a) proposed alternative(s) of doing research. It is proposed such procedures will help solve the justification problem.

The empirical data was collected before (in 2006, 2007) and after (in 2011) the current global economic crisis from managers and non-managers whose companies had to reorganise to survive. Using their experiences, the paper captures what individuals choose to contribute to collective tasks (as their chosen boundaries), what they see as the value of their contributions to deal with the link between the individual and collective level of functioning. In this sense employees take up active research functions, in relation to responding to outside influences. People's contributions should identify the link between individual and collective objectives, what resource develops from this linkage and what added value could be provided for future research, learning and development. The mapping provided in the justification of results is anticipated to provide its uniqueness in the added quality in that which has not been added yet. It is anticipated the use of employees' contributions forms part of a procedure to study companies from an 'in-here' position. The results as justified can then be classified as new forms of research through a new self-justificatory process. The link between individual and collective performances is treated as unique in a process of self-organisation. This could provide a resource, which is channelled towards the development of self-maintaining collectives (see also HEA UKPSF) that constitute "ways of establishing equivalences among beings" (Boltanski and Thēvenot 2006: 9) as a more inclusive, a more liberating form of organisation, of teaching and learning about research.

Justification has to contain a number of elements, as follows:
- Selecting organisations that show variety;
- Selecting management and non-management roles to inform the justificatory outcome(s);
- The situation(s) where participants' constructed experiences are interpreted as part of a 'meta' story of individuals contributing to a collective's task (Rorty 1991). The uniqueness of the results

means mapping has to be unique, i.e. undisturbed by external influences.

- The justificatory outcomes should demonstrate a procedure that produces collectives that 'strive' to increase their maintainability (i.e. sustainability) through their actions i.e. by increasing members' learning and adaptability. Such variety can act as a resource to solve problem situations in a coordinated way (-employees as producers). The quality of channelling variety resides in the way individuals' activities are transitioned onto collective objectives such that this transition maintains each level even when further challenged.
- Checking whether the name 'employees as producers' belongs to the activities being described helps minimise speculative interpretations through a self-checking process.
- Helping collectives to develop to the point where they have achieved maintainability between flexible individual contributions and collective performances to the point of recognising their progress as a self-recognisable, self-organising and self-justifying collective.

1.1   Historical context of justification

Justification can be traced back to the Protestant Reformation period (C16th.) as a major area of religious contention. Over time, it came to be associated with one's method of acting judiciously and therefore being 'atoned' with the law. Recently, theories of justification (e.g. coherence, reasoning, validity etc) have focused on whether our beliefs and values mirror 'a' or 'the' 'real' world in a depersonalised way in our quest for new forms of knowledge and understanding. The latter attempt to address the important question: 'how do we claim to know and understand what we know and understand?' Some of the main opponents of justification are "Bartley (in Bunge 1964)" and Popper (1934; 1959 trans.; 1980 ed.), who propose "critical rationalism". Over time, other proposals have varied between depersonalisation and situatedness. One could lay claims to discovery if it could be shown that something unique has been added from one's observations and the process justified. Certain discoveries may lead to inventions (e.g. of products, procedures).

Section 2 deals with challenges, 3 presents the justificatory arguments, while 4 accounts for its outcomes. Discussions are presented in section 5 and the conclusion in 6.

2   Challenges

To help simplify the justification problem other authors (see Lincoln and Guba 1985; Guba 1990; Reason and Hawkins 1988; Hacking 1981) have attempted to justify their work by their analogy with the notion of a paradigm as defined by Kuhn (1962). A group of people interact to solve problems until deviations appear that require 'revolutionary' solutions. It is claimed this procedure enhances further research competence and where deviations may appear the group 'strives' to justify the use of resources by comparing new findings with existing procedures and theories. Structural changes are needed in collecting (additional) observation material or a 'new' language is designed to solve a problem emerging from an 'older' problem (Whyte, Wilson and Wilson 1969). This could happen during stages considered 'deviations' to science and research when increased variety may pose further questions to already existing forms of knowing how, of teaching and learning to solve problems. This may lead to subversion and sabotage or to innovation and increase of collective competence (see Forsyth 1916; Chase and Simon 1973; Broadbent 1977; Kendall 1982; Frensch and Funke 1995).

2.1   Dealing with challenges

When organising material, some studies were noted close to the traditional Cartesian procedure (finding a single link between experiences and description through a reduction of differences of what the 'real' thing is) and others closer to the non-traditional Darwinian (or Darwinian-like) procedure (where behaviours being observed are closer to the procedure). The first is based on exhausting/saturating the link between experience and description (finding the widest set of observations and the most succinct representation). This implies creating a boundary around the experiences by studying them as if they were an object, so the link between 'object' and 'a' or 'the' 'reality' remains stable (see Star and Griesemer 1989). In the more complex Darwinian-type procedure, people construct their own boundaries and can react to or resist the procedure and its justification by creating more variations in their behaviour. Examples include 'wicked problems' (Hardin 1968; Rittel and Weber 1973).

To solve the problem of what justification procedure to adopt, it seems advisable to collect additional (primary) data (September to November 2011), particularly on companies that continue to be significantly challenged - to identify whether members' experiences show variety at complex behavioural levels (i.e. other than the level where variety is reduced and represented). Research procedures of how to study variety and resolve the justification problem are presented (see 2.1.1 and 2.1.2).

2.1.1   Procedure 1: Reducing variety

In that part of the literature studying people's behaviours, machine-like or Cartesian procedures dominate, relating people's actual behaviours to preferred end-states. The adopted procedure includes number variables, the relations between which constitute the problem. These tend to be used to define the parameters involved (Fayol 1949; Etzioni 1961; Beer 1966). Individuals are assumed either not able to choose whether to behave like the procedure, implying the possibility of prediction or to choose to do so (see case of the Hawthorne effect; Landsberger 1958 and Taylor 1947). Those involved may experience restrictions to their freedom and to what they can contribute, as they are treated as if they were object-like representations of 'reality'. When they do not, their behaviour is observed as variety or "overload" (de Zeeuw 1996: 19).

2.1.2   Procedure 2: Controlling variety

The search for a more uplifting procedure still fixates the behaviour of the controllers (e.g. representational research) in a non-inclusive way. For example, researchers may organise, develop and teach strategies that define, thereby control, the roles of participants, the potential links between the roles and what results are predicted.

Overstepping of roles (and variety) will, however, increase over time (and become better visible, e.g. via conflicts) when participants have to adapt their performance against the predicted outcomes. When this happens managers (as some researchers) may revert to procedure 1 (i.e. increase the control so contributions and behaviours are predictable and representable (Marx and Engels 1985 Ed.; "Weber (in Roth and Wittich1979 eds)"; Tjosvold 2007).

"Espoused values" (Schein 1985: 17, 244) make it possible for individuals to maintain variety by guarding some personal flexibility (Schein 1985: 17).

The 'value model' is sometimes claimed to help achieve the intended change in behaviour as the operational procedure constrains the former to 'espoused' values. However, many other values play a part in research and in learning, as they do in the continuation of a company or a university (e.g. the values of resisting the 'espoused' production procedure by constructing one's preferences). These preferences cannot be controlled unless through a more complex procedure.

3 Procedure 3: Self-justification

To deal with the problem of control in research-in-practice one needs a more complex process of justification. Not only are strategies of delineating members into a boundary with roles sufficient; the boundary itself becomes changeable in a wider group. It can be optimised to support the collective when performing activities. This makes the boundary the result of a system of cooperation (Gramsci 1971; Axelrod 1984). It identifies what members of a collective may see others in their environment to be doing and conveys to others what they too are doing (in terms of objectives and preferences). This type of process allows one to observe and report a wider range of values – allowing individual learning and contributions to be quite varied. Individuals become free to self-construct what they like to include or exclude. Members become aware of what their freedom is for (Jakupec and Garrick 2000).

3.1 Argument 1: On the level of research

Justifying research and striving for higher quality is not a trivial feat. Attempting to simplify the process is also not simple. Two arguments need clarification. Firstly there is need to change the research game from the traditionally representative and depersonalised, Cartesian type to the 'newer' Darwinian-like forms of organising. Here, situations and contexts do matter. Justifying by induction has been refuted most convincingly by Popper (1980) – except of course for the trivial case when what is being described contains only a finite number of elements, the links of which can be observed and represented. Difficulties arise when it is not known whether the number is infinite or finite. Not surprisingly, research based on reducing people's preferences (through representation) tended to have been among the earliest (see 2.1.1).

3.2   Argument 2: On the level of participants

Secondly, the Darwinian-like procedure suggests that the memories of con-tributors involved in change situations and how they might construct their preferences to bring the process of learning under their control be ex-plored– rather than observe or 'problematise' developments as an out-sider. Some associated difficulties are discussed.

Four sets of employees (51 in all) from 4 private-sector organisations in-tended to emphasise differences in roles and behaviours were studied. The organisations had these categories. Interviewees had different nationali-ties, from different geographical regions, with different values. They in-cluded people of European, African and Asian origins.

Questions were equally as varied and dealt, firstly, with changes in working practices and roles, how communication was carried out via what language construction. Secondly, they referred to constraints employees had experi-enced in performing tasks prior to and after the challenges, what form these had taken, how they had constructed their experiences of the pa-rameters of managerial relations. Respondents were invited to add any other constructions (of preferences) they considered vital to their interac-tions.

One of the difficulties is that people will be in the process of changing the construction of the internal language of the company by contributing to the discussions that the procedure generates. The previous language may not have gone and the new one may not have been fully constructed yet. There may be significant differences in the ways the differing languages are interpreted and understood by respondents, thereby increasing varia-tions. For example, responses from interviews may emphasise doubts about the challenges (and express feelings of loss), rather than reveal what is being constructed in the new company.

Challenges facing the companies are summarised hereunder:

Table 1: Summary of Company Challenges

In 2004, Longhurst faced the challenge of implementing its decision to expand to new counties in the UK. The company had to devise new divisions of labour, changes in roles and competences and had to induct new employees from European countries.
In 2005, Eden had to make 'reasonable adjustments' to their facilities in order to facilitate easy access and free movement of physically and/or mentally disabled people or those with other forms of disability. It had to face increasing resistance to some of its activities, e.g. building on brown or green sites.
In 2004, Laurens Patisserie faced a relatively fast increase in the demand for patisserie products (cakes and pies) from supermarkets. This consequently put pressure on employees' workloads. The company had to induct non-English staff, e.g. from European, East European, African and Middle Eastern origins.
In 2005, Prospects incorporated Connexions and had to manage the transfer from the 'old' company (Connexions) to the 'new' one (Prospects). This included adapting staff to Prospects' cultural norms and value systems, agreeing with union members and relocating staff.

When discussed with managers, they agreed challenges were varied and substantive. Responding to each challenge was seen as requiring considerable effort, implying individual and collective (re)-constructions and adaptations. It was expected employees would attempt to vary their contributions by constructing 'small' stories, linked to the ways they construct boundaries for a task and to the company's overall adaptation.

4 Employees' statements

Respondents' constructions initiated when the activities to deal with the challenges were announced. The story (and the six subsequent steps below) did not differ between the companies. The responses collected at the previous and recent interviews were treated as if they could be compared and after their comparison, appeared to tell the same complex story, except step 6. Yet, there has been some change from the 'old' to the new situation as employees started to interpret the new changes in behaviour as self-justified change and, therefore self-maintained change. Previously people were innovative because of the threats and because of management imposition to deal with the threats (see step 2 below); now they are innovative as a collective part of the new challenges (see step 6 below).

1.   There was an awareness of the need for changes, for example, from a situation of 'easy come and easy go before to get the work done

quicker... now, it is more professional and that has changed the chemistry of the company'.

2. Managers' imposition of discipline and punishment was considered tantamount to 'an invasion of employee territory'.

3. This led to employees' resistance of formalised relationships, where 'communication has become the biggest challenge'.

4. Employees were left 'feeling handcuffed' as they tried to develop 'training' initiatives for the collective good.

5. Employees feel the need to be valued but experience obstacles as 'to change the culture becomes extremely difficult' and 'the company has struggled to get staff from Newark'.

6. Employees begin to interpret tasks in their own way, to take initiatives that they do not report to the managers, in ways they consider beneficial to their company, as some employees wanted 'to have responsibility on the way things are going' and felt 'wound up if someone tells me what to do'. They felt 'able to make the department innovate even when the manager did not understand what was being done'.

At the sixth step participants begin to take their own initiatives. They direct their preferences as if to innovate and 'integrate learning' (Tinto 1975). These were part of their ways of dealing with the reorganisation's challenges. Now we can talk about the quality of the work as a different, somewhat special way of justifying research from the rather traditional, representational and Cartesian approach.

Responses suggest that workers can generate variety; that they are resilient despite attempts to control their preferences and are able to get around their managers by the sixth step. Step 6 is therefore better than step 2 in terms of portraying how a collective can deal with challenges to their survival. The form of reporting adopted here shows how to move from step 2 to 6 in a systematic way by developing interactions which have to satisfy 2 criteria:

1. The criteria of step 6 where people take initiatives thereby creating further variety;

2. A way of moving to step 6 systematically and justifying employees' actions. Employees can judge whether step 6 activities are good or bad and can change if needs be. The role of research is to support going to step 6 by supporting experiences and interactions in the direction of step 6 and possibly beyond.

This form of observing and reporting procedure seems sufficient to identify what employees produce when externally challenged. However it does not identify the way they look at the future and the way they take responsibility for events beyond their direct control. A more powerful, more complex procedure beyond step 6 is needed to see what can be achieved.

4.1   Employees as producers

Having identified the variety of behaviours and preferences that some interviewees have the ability to initiate around tasks and their usefulness, one might wish to identify some way or approach to stimulate these. Listening to a story might be effective. One objection would be, however, that a story usually does not self-justify the behaviour and the preferences it tells about, for example in terms of expected advantages. There is no indication, for example, that those who develop the required managerial behaviour in the story are less likely to be fired or relegated to less advantageous roles. The notion of employees as producers of their competence seems to respond to this problem. It identifies that those who develop certain behaviours attain some form of power – the power to vary their contributions and thereby justify their actions against threats, such as obstacles raised by the managers (or colleagues who subvert) or external ones such as acting as both carer and manager for people with complex disabilities (e.g. dementia). It might be objected again, unfortunately, that this does not provide the kind of justification that might be sought by managers or those who seek to control employees. It turns the story into a tool to achieve an objective (being able to do some activity). Something more uplifting as well as supportive is required: a more complex level of justification. One possibility would be to think of a procedure within which an understanding of how someone who actually wishes to enact the story by acting as a 'witness' (see Nevejan and Brazier 2011; Nevejan 2009), as well as create the competence this requires might proceed. Employees-as-producers capture this type of understanding and justification. When I repeatedly compared the procedure to the six-step-story developed from the interviews, I came to the same concept-employees-as-producers of their learning and adaptation.

'Employees-as-producers' indicates a new type of procedure (allowing for the construction of boundaries that contain far greater developmental preferences and variety than was previously possible in representational procedures or even in the 'values-model'). The first 2 procedures appear to lead to recognition systems in the Cartesian way (sections 2.1.1 and 2.1.2). If they can be shown to contain the relevant variety of experiences in daily life, they may allow for future recognition – if this leaves the procedure untouched (i.e. with no remaining variety). The procedure leading to the construction of employees-as-producers is intended to help create collectives that perform some task or action and have the freedom to vary their contributions and preferences. This is done through a process of self-organisation and self-justification, without their survival being disturbed or threatened or, if one wills, a collective becoming closed to further changes. This implies that the constructions and the contributions of the actors in the collectives constitute a resource for further learning and development (Kolb 1974; Fineman 2000; Bauman 2004). What constitutes people's idea of the collective task is recognised from the outside as a collective act even when the procedure adopted in its reporting shows differences in language used amongst participants and their interpretation of that language. This process seems to observe and is referred to as providing understanding of the idea that previously could be identified only dimly and partially by the story.

The procedure invented here serves as a double recognition system. Further checking may increase its quality. What seems to be of particular value is that the procedure contributes a valuable resource to support employees in a process of self-checking or self-justification that maintains collective survival. The concept allows to identify what contributes to its own viable implementation in organisational situations and hence when it has achieved high quality: i.e. when the collective stays undisturbed by further challenges. This characteristic makes it highly attractive as an alternative to the traditional procedure (see sections 2.1.1 and 2.1.2). Implementing the procedure implies that people (as participating members of organisations) become able to choose what objective to construct. This makes checking the concept part of its implementation: one cannot de-velop a procedure that constructs an object function if one does not inter-act and ensure that individual activities help realise the collective act. The procedure contributes in two valuable ways: it serves as a constraint on what people are able to contribute to tasks and facilitates the effective-ness and changeability of their contributions when considered necessary. Therefore, it provides a framework for the observation and the language for reporting of the behaviour in local, context-dependent situations that goes beyond those of representations, stories and interactions. It is self-justificatory.

5 Discussion

The interviews are interpreted as presentations of employee experiences and as expressions of a more general linguistic structure. The variety of the responses was taken to indicate that employees were varying their contri-butions and thereby adapting individual preferences to collective reorgani-sations, "acting as representatives in their turn" (Boltanski and Thévenot 2006: 3). The six-step-story supports and is supported by some elements of the literature (e.g. on management's attempts to reduce differences, on individual and collective learning and development and self-justification). The procedure reported what direction the statements suggested that em-ployees wished to modify the constructions of their experiences. Respon-dents could be said to have 'researcher-ship' and 'knowing-in-action' (Schon 1983). To enable this type of act, the statements were structured and reported in a language that tells the 'meta'-story of how to invent a procedure that helps justify combining preferences.

In addition to the procedure reported here, other approaches have been developed to approximate the justification of what one is exploring in case it is unknown what amount of individual and collective preferences is in-volved. These may be categorised into three types. The first one is to con-sider the procedure's internal coherence. If, for example, a next step only makes use of a previous step and nothing is added from outside the step, the results are considered justified. This often is called the (a posteriori) utility approach (Brody 1984; Finlay 2008). The second is to consider exter-nal coherence. This means that research is taken to add something 'wider' to an initial problem area, e.g. a frame via which to identify related data, or a pattern to predict or anticipate new phenomena, or an environment that needs to be controlled to be able to achieve a procedure's objectives. This is often called justification by design. The third is to position the work done in terms of some 'debates', or of what seems close, 'traditions'. This type of justification raises the additional problem of the entanglement of the languages being studied – the language of its coordination and the language of the debates. These include discussions whether the results are due to the use of quantitative or qualitative methods, whether they can be used with some confidence even if the design is executed with limited resources, whether what is added represents 'a' or 'the' 'reality' and so on. None guarantees that checking will be exhaustive as "defections are not avoided" (de Zeeuw 1996: 20). The alternative research proposition developed in the paper is a form of language, whose structure determines or produces the research content. If research is conducted following step 2, it would produce data or reports for management to impose on employees further, thereby help to justify the curtailing of employees' variety. At step 6, this will not suffice as differences in interpretations are permitted while still allowing space for collective action. The procedure leading to employees-as-producers (post step 6) was found to have sufficiently mirrored both the name as well as the naming of the variety that employees choose to contribute to collective performances for their maintainability.

6   Conclusion

To meet the paper's objective, the procedure I invented included arranging for interviews with people familiar with at least some organisations experiencing radical restructuring. The procedure and its elements were identified as were possible outcomes and checking for quality. Combining these elements as an alternative way to study organisations from a situated perspective is proposed. Further work is required to deal with emerging multi-faceted variety from a group of interacting participants (e.g. higher education policy-makers, tutors, university authorities and students, managers and non-managers) especially where and when the division of labour, roles and interactions have been loosened to a point where a larger range of conflicting values, opinions, myths and assumptions become operational. Further work is also considered necessary to capture the next level of research development beyond the sixth step of operational procedure. In other words, what happens to participants (e.g. employees-as-producers etc) once they have achieved the learning, the skills for collective 'researcher-ship' competence? On an individual level, what (or who?) do I become? These, and related questions/problems could provide the bases for more complex research formulations and further research on the processes of research, processes of discovery and problem-solving as well as processes of self-justification. The work continues...

References

Axelrod, R. (1984) The evolution of cooperation, Basic Books, New York.

Bauman, Z. (2004) Work, consumerism and the new poor, Open University Press, Maidenhead.

Beer, S. (1966) Decision and Control, Wiley, New York.

Boltanski, L. and Thēvenot, L. (2006) Justification: economies of worth (C. Porter trans.), Princeton University Press, Princeton.

Broadbent, D.E. (1977) 'Levels, hierarchies and the locus of control', Quarterly journal of experimental psychology, Vol. 29, pp 181-201.

Brody, P.J. (1984) 'In Search of instructional utility: A function-based approach to pictorial research', Instructional Science, Vol. 13, No. 1: pp 47-61.

Bunge, M. (1964 ed.) The Critical Approach to Science and Philosophy, The Free Press of Glencoe.

Chase, W.G. and Simon, H.A. (1973) 'Perception in chess', Cognitive Psychology, Vol. 4, pp 55-81.

Darwin, C. (1858) 'On the tendency of species to form varieties and on the perpetuation of varieties and species by natural means of selection', Journal of the proceedings of the Linnean Society of London, Zoology Vol. 3: pp 46-50.

Descartes, R. (1837) Discourse on Method [Translated from French: Discours de la mêthode], Penguin Books, London.

De Zeeuw, G. (1996) 'Three Phases of Science: A Methodological Exploration', Centre for Systems and Information Sciences, University of Humberside, ISBN186050 250 0

Etzioni, A. (1961) A Comparative Analysis of Complex Organisations: on power, involvement and their correlates, Free Press, New York.

Fayol, H. (1949) General and Industrial Management, Pitman Publishing, New York.

Fineman, S. (2000) Emotions in Organisations, Sage, London.

Finlay, S.M. (2008) 'Towards profitability: a utility approach to the credit-scoring problem', Journal of Operational Research Society, Vol. 59: pp 921-931.

Forsyth, P.T. (1917) The Justification of God: Lectures for Wartime on a Christian Theodicy, Independent Press, London.

Frensch, P. and Funke, F. (1995) Complex problem-solving: the European Perspective, Laurence Earlbaum Associates, Hillsdale, New Jersey.

Gramsci, A. (1971 Ed.) Selections from the prison notebooks of Antonio Gramsci (Q. Hoare and G. Nowell-Smith eds. and trans.), Lawrence and Wishart, London.

Guba, E.G. (1990) The paradigm dialogue, Sage, Newbury.

Hacking, I. (1981) Scientific revolutions, Oxford University Press, New York.

Hardin, G. (1968) 'The Tragedy of the Commons', Science, Vol. 162, No. 3859: pp 1243-1248.

Jakupec, V. and Garrick, J. (2000 ed.) Flexible Learning, Human Resource and Organisational Development, Routledge, London.

Kendall, P.C. (1982 ed.) Advances in cognitive behavioural research and therapy
(Vol. 1), Academic Press, New York.

Kolb, D. (1974) Experiential Learning: Experience as the source of Learning and
Development, Prentice Hall, London.

Kuhn, T.S. (1962) The Structure of Scientific Revolutions, University of Chicago
Press, Chicago.

Landsberger, H.A. (1958) Hawthorne revisited, Ithaka, Cornell University.

Lincoln, Y. and Guba, E.G. (1985) Naturalist inquiry, Sage Publications, Newbury
Park, California.

Marx, K. and Engels, F. (1848) The Communist Manifesto, (S. Moore 1985 ed. and
trans.) Penguin, Harmondsworth.

Miller, D. (2007) 'Overcoming the justification addiction', Lecture delivered at University of Bergen, Socrates-Erasmus 2006/07 Teacher Mobility Programme,
funded by Commission of European Communities.

Nevejan, C. (2009) 'Witnessed presence and the YUTPA framework' Sprouts,
PsychNology Journal, Vol. 7, No. 1: pp 59-76. ISSN1535-6078.

Nevejan, C. and Brazier, F. (2011) 'Witnessed Presence in Merging Realities in
Healthcare Environments', Studies in Computational Intelligence, Vol. 326: pp
201-227. doi 10.1007/978-3-642-16095-0_11

Popper, K.R. (1980 Ed.) The Logic of Scientific Discovery, Unwin Hyman, New York.

Reason, P. and Hawkins, P. (1988) Human Inquiry in Action: Developments in New
Paradigm Research, Sage, London.

Rittel, H. and Weber, M. (1973) Dilemmas in a General Theory of Planning, Policy
Studies, Vol. 4: pp 155-169.

Rorty, R. (1991) Consequences of Pragmatism, Harvester, London.

Roth, G. and Wittich, C. (1978 Eds.) Economy and Society: an outline of interpretive
sociology, University of California Press, Berkeley.

Schein, E.H. (1985) Organizational Culture and Leadership, Jossey-Bass, San Fran-
cisco.

Schon, D.A. (1983) The reflective practitioner: how professionals think in action,
Arena, Aldershot.

Star, S.L. and Griesemer, J.R. (1989) 'Institutional Ecology, Translations and Boundary Objects, Amateurs and Professionals in Berkeley's Museum of Vertebrate
Zoology', Social Studies of Science 19, 1907-39, pp 387-420, doi: 10.
101177/030631289019003001

Taylor, F. (1947) Scientific Management, Harper and Brothers, New York.

The UK Professional Standards Framework, The Higher Education Academy, The
Higher Education Academy, York, UK.

Tinto, V. (1975) 'Dropout from Higher Education: A Theoretical Synthesis of recent
Research', Review of Education Research, Vol. 45, pp 89-125.

Tjosvold, D. (2007) 'Cooperative and Competitive Goal Approach to Conflict: Accomplishments and Challenges', Applied Psychology, Vol. 47, No. 3: pp 285-313.

Vahl, M. (1997) 'Doing research in the social domain: concepts and criteria'. In Systems for Sustainability, People, Organisations and Environments, Stowell, F.A., Ison, I.R., Plenum Press, New York/London.

Whyte, L.L.; Wilson, A.G. and Wilson, D. (1969) Hierarchical Structures, American Elsevier, New York.

Researching the Outliers: Bridging the Rigor-Relevance Divide in Management Research With CIT?

Karl Joachim Breunig and Line Christoffersen
School of Business, Oslo and Akershus University College, Oslo, Norway
Originally published in ECRM (2014) Conference Proceedings

Editorial Commentary

The paper addresses an important question in business and management research, i.e. the question of scientific rigour and practical relevance in the area of study. The challenge that the paper seeks to deal with is how to integrate what the authors conceptualise as practically relevant 'outliers' in business and management with scientific rigour and application so as to overcome the rigour-relevance research conundrum. It is proposed that outliers can contribute twofold: by assisting in theory building as well as providing potential solutions to problems in business and management practice. The Critical Incident Technique (or CIT) is suggested as a tool to enhance bridging the divide between scientific rigour and practical business and management relevance. Ways of collecting, presenting and making sense of narratives within a framework and provided as part of what is being proposed. The methodology has been adequately developed. However, the paper could have benefited from a strengthening of the data element so as to further demonstrate how the 'outliers' have been collected as part of the process of bridging the rigour-relevance problem in business and management research.

Abstract: Management science is an applied field of research; however, it is a need for an extension of methods to increase the practical relevance of its findings. This paper aims at bridging the divide suggested by the rigour-relevance debate on research methods in management sciences. Research-based knowledge, whether aiming at theory development or practical utility, need to abide to strict scientific procedures and criteria to be trustworthy. The challenge is that practical relevance and scientific rigour represent different logics, were researchers often disregard the knowledge most valuable to practitioners as outliers. Hence, we raise the question: How can management science methods be fused with insight from other scientific disciplines to overcome the rigour-relevance divide? We suggest that management science can increase relevance by rigorously handling outliers instead of washing them out since the identification of outliers can potentially contribute to both theory development and problem solving in practice. Diverse fields have successfully deployed Critical Incidents Technique (CIT) to ensure both theory development and as a vehicle to identify and resolve specific problems. CIT is designed to capture and explain the occurrence of outliers. Critical incidents are unique situations analysed to identify the cause and effects of these incidents in context. We suggest that using CIT can increase the practical relevance of management research without compromising scientific standards. In this paper, we extend extant qualitative research methodology within the management field by fusing it with core properties from CIT. We present a canvas explaining how to design, collect, analyse and present narrative knowledge from CIT based workshops. Our suggested framework utilise CIT to provide unique and context specific data that can be utilised both in inductive theory building as well as being useful for management in practice.

Keywords: critical incidents technique, inductive theory building, management research, outliers, rigor-relevance debate, storytelling.

1 Introduction

Management is a broad an applied research field. Even so, in our work as researchers, we have often come across practitioners who disregard popular management research agendas as irrelevant, too general or too abstract. Researchers on the other hand, often discount the knowledge most valuable to practitioners as outliers. An outlier is an observation point that is distant from other observations in a set of data. The distance can be ascribed to variability in measurements and thus be considered as an experimental error. However, discarding outliers are more problematic in the context of open systems, such as organizations, where entirely new phenomena can emerge from its contextual complexity. In an organizational context, outliers can be early indications of new emerging phenomena that can prove valuable to both theory development and practical use. Research based knowledge needs to abide to strict scientific procedures and criteria. Thus, there is a need to scrutinize the method applied in management science to assess how it can simultaneously be relevant to practice, have impact by addressing interesting research questions, and abide by scientific norms and standards to be trustworthy. However, one can argue that research and practice inhabit fundamentally different social systems (Kierser and Leiner, 2009). Moreover, practical relevance and scientific rigour represent different logics; where science seeks to identify repetitive patterns; practitioners are more interested in novel practices or unique ideas. In addition some researchers have addressed the need for improved attention to research with impact as many research articles are hardly ever cited by other researchers (Pettigrew, 2011).

This paper aims at bridging the divide suggested by the rigour-relevance debate on research methods in management sciences (e. g. Kieser and Leiner, 2009, Hodgkinson and Rousseau, 2009, Kieser, 2011, Gopinath and Hoffman, 1995, Starkey and Madan, 2001, Rynes et al., 2001, Vermeulen, 2005). Methods applied in management research should have impact on the production of new scientific knowledge as well as be relevant for practitioners especially in an applied field as management science. Thus, there is a need for an extended repertoire of methods to adhere to the specific, context dependent and the unique. We suggest that research methods adhering better to outliers potentially can provide a bridge for the rigour-relevance divide. Hence, we address the research question: *How can management science methods be fused with insight from other scientific disciplines to overcome the rigour-relevance divide?* Our contribution is a framework fusing extant qualitative methods in management research with Critical Incidents Technique (CIT).

CIT was developed by Flanagan (1954) as a method in clinical psychology as means to both produce diagnosis and develop diagnostic categories. We suggest that the utilization of CIT can increase the practical relevance of management research without compromising scientific standards. John Flanagan (1954) defined CIT as "a set of procedures for collecting direct observations of human behaviour in such a way as to facilitate their potential usefulness in solving practical problems and developing broad psychological principles". CIT have since been successfully deployed in diverse fields from marketing to medical research as a vehicle to produce both contextual data relevant for practice as well as a basis for inductive theory building. We suggest that the introduction of CIT to management research methods can provide a potential bridge to the rigour-relevance divide.

In this paper we extend extant inductive theory building research methodology within the management field (Eisenhardt, 1989, Graebner et al., 2012, Flyvbjerg, 2006) by fusing it with core properties from CIT, especially its ability to handle narratives (Burns et al., 2000, Westbrook et al., 2007, Andrews et al., 2009, Helkkula and Pihlström, 2010, Kaye and Jacobson, 1999). We address how to collect, analyse and present narrative knowledge from CIT based workshops. The contribution of this paper is to present a platform upon which to provide relevant research with high varsity of its data that enable researchers and practitioners to handle outliers better.

The paper is structured in three main parts. First, we present the rigour-relevance debate. Second, we present CIT, placing it within the narrative strand of organizational research, and explain how other research traditions deploy CIT in both theory building and practical use. Third, we explain how fusing established qualitative research methodology, such as case study design, storytelling method, and participatory action research, with CIT can provide a bridge for the rigour-relevance divide and introduce the Critical Incidents Canvas (CITC) as an integrated framework to reveal and handle outliers.

2 The rigour-relevance divide in management research

Several authors have addressed potential future directions of management science and related fields such as strategic management (Gopinath and Hoffman, 1995, Løwendahl and Revang, 1998), organization studies (Pettigrew et al., 2001, Foss et al., 2012) and accounting (Guthrie et al., 2012). Bartunek (2003) addressed how management research could be made more interesting, and refer to a survey made for the Academy of Management concluding; "that it was both possible and desirable to raise the proportion of articles published that are regarded as important, competently executed, and really interesting". However, with respect to the direction of an applied field of research Bartunek et al. (2006) state that "the first criterion by which people judge anything they encounter, even before deciding whether it is true or false, is whether it is interesting or boring". Pettigrew (2011) also, call for increased scholarship with impact, addressing the disinterest other researchers have for much of the current research published. Many researchers complain that there is an increasing challenge to get companies to engage in research collaboration and that they struggle to access interesting data. Pettigrew (1990, 274) states that choosing a research site and gaining access to it, is a matter of "planned opportunism", and that research collaboration will only occur if managers understand how it will benefit their firm.

These issues touch upon a prolonged debate in the management literature about the rigor-relevance gap in extant research modelling. Research is expected to be conducted in a systematic and transparent fashion, providing objective measures and rigorous conclusions. This is in contrast to the reality experienced by practitioners, which is much about making sense of complexity, sorting out multiple options, or understanding how important stakeholders respond to the firms' actions. Indeed, there are fundamental difference between the motivation for research and practice: Researchers are looking for repetitiveness as opposed to practitioners who are searching for the specific or unique. Many researchers are overly attending to their R squared, and consequently they need to get the outliers washed out of their data sets in order to publish.

Several studies maintain that the rigor–relevance gap in management research is fundamentally unbridgeable because researchers and the researched inhabit separate social systems (Kieser and Leiner, 2009, Kieser, 2011, Kieser and Alexander, 2005). However, Hodgkinson and Rousseau (2009) contradict this idea and provide a number of counter-illustrations of work where researchers in collaboration with practitioners have generated knowledge that is both socially useful and academically rigorous. In particular Gopinath and Hoffman (1995) emphasize that it is important for strategy research to have practical relevance given its professional orientation and conclude that the agendas of researchers and practitioners should be viewed as complementary. They survey CEO's of major US corporations to reveal a practitioners' agenda for the field and compare the results with an agenda generated among academics. Compared to academics, CEOs emphasize operating issues; disagree on the priority of strategic issues; and are generally unfamiliar with research-based journals. Starkey and Madan (2001) elaborates the complementary agendas and explain how there is beneficial to align the two social systems. They identify a need for stakeholding, a new form of research partnership and research training, affecting various aspects of the research and dissemination process. This idea about increased interaction between researchers and practitioners are supported by Rynes et al. (2001), and Polzer et al. (2009) recommending that a "full-cycle" approach to conducting research can help organizational scholars increase the relevance of their work. One approach to obtaining this research partnership is action research (Greenwood and Levin, 1998) entailing close collaboration between researchers and the practitioners. Rather than conduction research *on*, action research, imply conducting research *with* the participating practitioners through co-generative learning. Co-generative learning is a facilitated process of learning between the researchers and the organisational stakeholders (Elden and Levin, 1991). The outcomes of co-generated learning are rich data, validated by the practitioners, which can be utilized in inductive theory building.

An approach to inductive theory building is the grounded theory building (Glaser and Strauss, 1967, Glaser, 1998, Strauss and Corbin, 1994, Strauss and Corbin, 1998). This case-based method involves the continuous comparison of collected data and theory, and results in theoretical categories based solely on evidence i.e. from thick descriptions (Geertz, 1973). There are no consensus on how to conduct case study research (Barratt et al., 2011), however, Siggelkow (2007) suggests that single case studies should present a "talking pig", that is a powerful and unique example of the phenomenon the research is centred around. The outliers washed out of many data samples can potentially represent "talking pigs" suitable to make a case story persuasive. An example could be the Hawthorn studies (Mayo, 1933). The "talking pig" of this classic study is the counter intuitive effect on performance when controlling for decreased lighting. Imagine if the Hawthorn researchers had stopped with the positive effect of light on performance and discarded the last part as an outlier. We suggest that an extension of methods to capture and utilize outliers for rigorous and relevant research can be achieved with insights from Critical Incidents Techniques (CIT).

3   CIT and the narrative strand of organizational research

Flanagan (1954) introduced critical incident technique (CIT) describing several studies with focus on mapping critical incidents. The technique was originally developed to improve procedures for selection and classification of US Air Force personnel during the Second World War. Later CIT was further developed to map officer's actions in combat. Experienced soldiers where asked to report observed incidents displaying officers conduct that they found particularity relevant for the success or failure of a mission. The examinations where always concluded with the question "describe the officers actions. What did he do?" Thousands of incidents where collected and analysed and the research resulted in categories describing critical conditions for good leadership conduct in combat situations. Flanagan (1954: 327) defined incidents as "any observable human activity that is sufficiently complete in itself to permit interferences and predictions to be made about the person performing the act. To be critical, an incident must occur in a situation where the purpose or intent of the act seems fairly clear to the observer and where its consequences are sufficiently definite to leave little doubt concerning its effects."

In the intervening years, CIT has proved itself a widely used qualitative research method being used across a variety of research fields. From the 1940's and well into the 1990's the method was utilized within the field of psychology and medical profession, for example utilized in hospitals to map critical incidents (Ivarsson et al., 2005, Arvidsson and Fridlund, 2005 , Andrew and Whyte, 2004 , Aveyard, 2005, Silen-Lipponen et al., 2004 , Fagerskiold et al., 2003 , Angelides, 2001, Ölvingson, 2002 , Query and Wright, 2003). The method was also used in organization studies, and focused mainly on factors affecting the performance of managers and employees. More recently the method have been adopted by researchers within the fields of marketing and service management (Edvardsson and Roos, 2001, Edvardsson and Strandvik, 1999, Edvardsson and Strandvik, 2000, Flanagan, 1954). Although it is a qualitative research method, "... the CIT was initially posed as a scientific tool to help uncover existing realities or truths so they could be measured, predicted, and ultimately controlled within the realm of job and task analysis" (Butterfield et al. 2005: 482). The research tradition of the day was underpinned by a positivist tradition (Chell 1998), however, from the mid 1990s there is also an increase of CIT within phenomenology (Symon and Cassell, 2004).

The advantages of the CIT are its non-academic and action-oriented approach (Hettlage and Steinlin 2006). CIT is a useful tool for a) collecting data for planning, assessments, base line studies, fact-findings (and applied research, usually within a wider research framework, e. g. action research), and b) reflecting on professional practice (Hettlage and Steinlin 2006). Critical incidents tell us what happened, but no *why* it happened. The possible causes are to be developed together with the interview partners. The chief value of the CIT for management studies resides in its potential to help researchers understand the related behaviours critical to complex situations and proceedings in and between all kinds of groupings (ibid).

According to Flanagan (1954), the CIT has five major steps:

3.1 Ascertaining the general aims of the activity being studied

Understanding the general aim of the activity is intended to answer two questions: 1) what is the objective of the activity; and 2) what is the person who engages in the activity expected to accomplish?

3.2 Making plans and setting specifications

Flanagan believed that four specifications needed to be decided upon:
- defining the types of situations to be observed,
- determining the situation's relevance to the general aim,
- understanding the extent of the effect the incident has on the general aim, and
- deciding who will be observing (e.g. experts in the field, supervisors, consumers of the product or service, or individuals performing the activity).

3.3 Collecting the data

This can be done in several ways, such as having individuals report from memory about incidents that occurred in the past. Although Flanagan preferred expert observers to gather data, he was also pragmatic enough to realize this was not always possible. He spent some time gathering evidence supporting the accuracy of recalled incidents, suggesting that accuracy can be deducted from the level of full, precise details given by the participant. Flanagan advocated four ways of obtaining recalled data in the form of critical incidents: 1) individual interviews, 2) group interviews, 3) questionnaires, and 4) record forms – recording details of incidents either in narrative form or by placing a check mark beside an activity on a pre-existing list of the most likely activities to be observed. Flanagan stressed that in a CIT study the sample size is not determined by the number of participants, but rather the number of critical incidents observed or reported, and whether the incidents represent adequate coverage of the activity being studied.

3.4   Analysing the data

The purpose of this stage is to create a categorization scheme that summarizes and describes the data in a useful manner, while at the same time "sacrificing as little as possible of their comprehensiveness, specificity and validity" (Flanagan 1954: 344). This necessitates navigating through three primary stages: 1) determining the frame of reference, which generally arises from the use that is to be made of the data (e.g. the frame of reference for evaluating on-the-job effectiveness is quite different that required for selection or training purposes), 2) formulating the categories (an inductive process), and 3) determining the level of specificity or generality to be used in reporting the data.

According to Serrat (2010), the analysis of a critical incident describes the setting in which an incident occurred, the behaviour (including the attitudes, emotions, skills, knowledge, and resources) of the people involved, and the outcome or result of the behaviour. The analysis brings cognitive, affective, and behavioural dimensions together, touching both the content of what is learned and the process of learning.

When analysing a critical incident reflective individuals ask questions like (Serrat 2010):

- Why did I view the original situation in that way?
- What assumptions about it did I make?
- How else could I have interpreted it?
- What other action(s) might I have taken that could have been more helpful?
- What will I do if I face with a similar situation again?

3.5   Interpreting the data and reporting the results

Flanagan suggested researchers start by examining the previous four steps to determine what biases have been introduced by the procedures used and what decisions have been made. He advocated that limitations be discussed, the nature of judgment be made explicit, and the value of the results be emphasized in the final report.

4   Bridging the rigor-relevance divide with CIT

In order to bridge the rigour-relevance gap we suggest that facilitating close research partnerships that over time enable the researcher and practitioner to detect and make sense of outliers. We suggest an integrated framework, extending extant qualitative methods with CIT and storytelling methods (see figure 1).

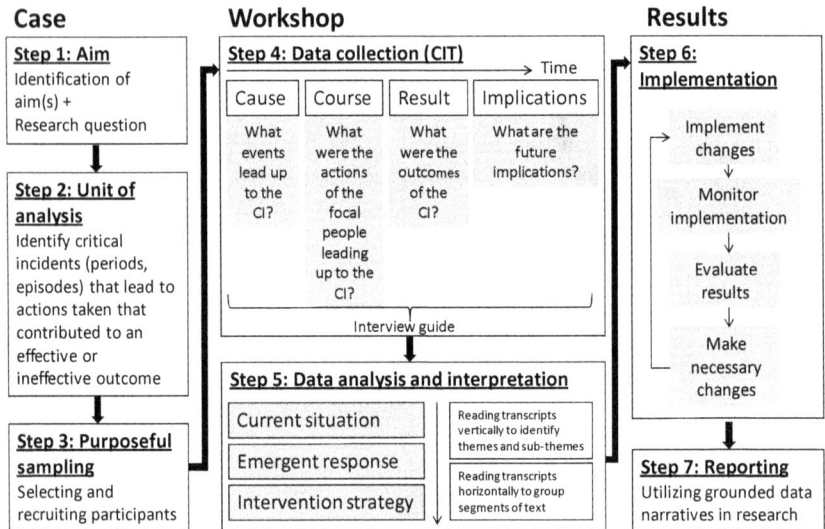

Figure 1: The critical incidents technique canvas

The suggested Critical Incidents Technique Canvas (CITC) consist of 7 steps, where the first three steps are underpinned by case study methodology (e. g. Eisenhardt and Graebner, 2007, Graebner et al., 2012, Flyvbjerg, 2011, Yin, 1994). The first three steps are:

- Step 1. Aim: Address the research goal(s) with special emphasis on identifying problems, vulnerability or a crisis with appropriate research question(s).
- Step 2. Unit of analysis: Identify critical incidents (periods, episodes) that lead to actions taken that contributed to an effective or ineffective outcome (e.g. Serrat, 2001).
- Step 3. Purposeful sampling: Relates to research design and the ability to purposively select and recruit participants (e. g. Eisenhardt, 1989, Flyvbjerg, 2006).

The subsequent two next steps are related to interaction with practitioners in workshops. The workshop is designed as a storytelling session (Ljungberg and Bergquist, 2005). The storytelling sessions are similar to focus groups (Krueger and Casey, 2000). The idea is to document through these sessions what really matters in the context. Accelerate the research process by making many voices heard simultaneously. The storytelling method is distinguished from semi-structured or structured interviews by a more explorative framework. The researcher has not predefined all issues that are to be addressed so the format enables themes that are viewed as important by the participants to emergence. The findings from the story-telling sessions can be utilized for qualitative interview guides, qualitative questioners, or as data directly. Collected anecdotes can be utilized organizationally i.e. to elaborate and give context to quantifiable reporting. The two subsequent steps are:

- Step 4. Data collection: Facilitation of storytelling sessions to retrieve judgement situations from memory (Edvardsson and Roos, 2001) as well as CIT (Edvardsson, 1992).
- Step 5. Data analysis and interpretation: Involve inductive analysis (Polit and Beck, 2004) with two levels of reading research transcripts; vertically - to identify themes and sub-themes; horizontally to identify grouping segments.

Finally, the last steps involve the results of the research partnership. It is in these two steps that the integrated framework intends to deliver output that is relevant both to the research agenda and give data that is relevant to practice. The two final steps are:

- Step 6. Implementation: Involve the design and implementation of potential changes suggested by the research partnership. The implementation is underpinned by the ideas of participatory action research where researcher and practitioner experience co-generative learning.
- Step 7. Reporting: Seek to overcome challenges getting published with qualitative data (Pratt, 2009). Utilizing grounded data narratives from this approach provide longitudinal and rich data that can be utilized for inductive theory building. In particular with respect to the identification of new theoretical categories stemming from observations of small but critical incidents.

The framework explains how research partnerships (Rynes et al., 2001) and stakeholding (Starkey and Madan, 2001) in a "full-cycle" approach (Polzer et al., 2009) can be obtained to overcome the rigor-relevance divide.

5   Conclusion

We set out to bridge the rigour-relevance divide by suggesting a frame-work fusing extant qualitative methods in management research with Critical Incidents Technique (CIT) and thereby enabling researchers to handle outliers as a vantage point in inductive theory building research. The framework we introduce is the Critical Incidents Technique Canvas integrating extant methods of case study, action research and co-generative learning as well as inductive interpretation and analysis with CIT and story-telling method. The framework provide management researcher with a tool to identify and handle outliers. We suggest that both scientific rigour and practical relevance can be achieved with an improved ability to handle outliers in management research methods when fused with CIT.

The theoretical framework suggested has its limitations. Although using storytelling strengthens validity because data is collected from the infor-mants' perspective using narratives in his or her own words, CIT relies on incidents being judged as critical, being remembered and correctly re-ported. A person's memory has an inclination to remember incidents that happened recently because these are easier to recall. Further, there is always the risk of informants only reporting incidents that reflect positively on themselves, and only reporting rare **events** (everyday issues may be missed). Getting accuracy of critical incident data thus warrants an experienced facilitator and moderator who are able to add follow-up questions and by probing, arrive at a thick descriptions and understanding of critical incidents. Researchers and practitioners must agree on the interpretation from the CIT and find a common platform before entering into the implementations phase using participatory action research. En in depth description of how this platform is developed is necessary to strengthen the validity of the research.

A common critic towards both CIT and participatory action research is that the results are situation specific and that the findings have limited generalizability. Suggestions for further research would be to perform a cross-case analysis to strengthen both reliability and generalizability. The researcher(s) should also provide a detailed description of the research process for the reader to be able to judge the applicability of the research.
Our suggested canvas can be time consuming. First, collecting enough number of incidents may take time. Second, the categorization process for CIT data is painstaking and slow. Third, even if participatory action re-

search is a powerful tool that empower and reflect ways of knowing, being and doing that are culturally endemic to the organization; results from participatory action research can be slow since, by nature, the research process has no set end date.

References

Andrew, J. & Whyte, F. (2004) The experiences of district nurses caring for people receiving palliative chemotherapy. *International Journal of Palliative Nursing* 10, 110-8.

Andrews, D. H., Hull, T. D. & Donahue, J. A. (2009) Storytelling as an Instructional Method: Definitions and Research Questions. *Interdisciplinary Journal of Problem-based Learning,* 3, 6-29.

Angelides, P. (2001) The development of an efficient technique for collecting and analyzing qualitative data: The analysis of critical incidents. *International Journal of Qualitative Studies in Education,* 14, 429-442.

Arvidsson, B. & Fridlund, B. (2005) Factors influencing nurse supervisor competence: a critical incident analysis study. *Journal of Nursing Management* 13, 231.

Aveyard, H. (2005) Informed consent prior to nursing care procedures. *Nursing Ethics,* 12, 19-29.

Barratt, M., Choi, T. Y. & Mei, L. (2011) Qualitative case studies in operations management: Trends, research outcomes, and future research implications. *Journal of Operations Management,* 29 329-342.

Bartunek, J. M. (2003) A dream for the academy: 2002 Presidential Address. *Academy of Management Review,* 28, 198-203.

Bartunek, J. M., Rynes, S. L. & Ireland, D. R. (2006) What makes management research interesting, and why does it matter. *Academy of Management Journal,* 49, 9-15.

Burns, A. C., Williams, L. A. & Maxham Iii, J. (2000) Narrative text biases attending the critical incidents technique. *Qualitative Market Research: An International Journal,* 3, 178-186.

Butterfield, L. D., Borgen, W. A., Amundson, N. E., & Malio, A.-S. T. 2005. Fifty years of the critical incident technique: 1954-2004 and beyond. *Qualitative Research,* 5(4): 475–497

Edvardsson, B. (1992) Service Breakdowns: A Study of Critical Incidents in an Airline International Journal of Service Industry Management, 3, 17-29.

Edvardsson, B. & Roos, J. (2001) Critical Incident Techniques - Towards a framework for analysing the criticality of critical incidents. *International Journal of Service Industry Management,* 12, 251-268.

Edvardsson, B. & Strandvik, T. (1999) *Criticality of Critical Incidents in Customer Relationships,* Wiesbaden, Deutscher Universitäts Verlag.

Edvardsson, B. & Strandvik, T. (2000) Is a Critical Incident Critical for a Customer Relationship? . *Managing Service Quality,* 10, 82-91.

Eisenhardt, K. (1989) Building theories from case study research. *Academy of Management Review,* 14, 532-550.

Eisenhardt, K. & Graebner, M. (2007) Theory building from cases: Opportunities and challenges. *Academy of Management Journal,* 50, 25-32.

Fagerskiold, A., Timpka, T. & Ek, A. C. (2003) The view of the child health nurse among mothers. *Scandinavian Journal of Caring Sciences* 17, 160-8.

Flanagan, J. C. (1954) The critical incident technique. *Psychological Bulletin,* 51, 327- 358.

Flyvbjerg, B. (2006) Five misunderstandings about case-study research. *Qualitative Inquiry,* 12 219-245.

Flyvbjerg, B. (2011) Case Study. *In:* Denzin, N. K. & Lincoln, Y. S. (eds.) *The Sage Handbook of Qualitative Research.* 4th ed. Thousand Oaks, CA: Sage.

Foss, N. J., Heimeriks, K. H., Winter, S. G. & Zollo, M. (2012) A Hegelian Dialogue on the Micro-Foundations of Organizational Routines and Capabilities. *European Management Review,* 9, 173-197.

Geertz, C. (1973) Thick Description. *The Interpretation of Cultures: Selected Essays.* New York: Basic Books.

Glaser, B. (1998) *Doing Grounded Theory - Issues and Discussions*, Sociology Press.

Glaser, B. G. & Strauss, A. L. (1967) *The Discovery of Grounded Theory: Strategies for Qualitative Research.,* New York, Aldine Publishing Company.

Gopinath, C. & Hoffman, R. C. (1995) The Relevance of Strategy Research: Practitioner and Academic Viewpoints*. *Journal of Management Studies,* 32, 575-594.

Graebner, M. E., Martin, J. A. & Roundy, P. T. (2012) Qualitative data: Cooking without a recipe. *Strategic Organization,* 10, 276–284.

Greenwood, D. J. & Levin, M. (1998) *Introduction to Action Research. Social Research for Social Change* Sage Publication.

Guthrie, J. P., Ricceri, F. & Dumay, J. (2012) Reflections and projections: A decade of Intellectual Capital Accounting Research. *The British Accounting Review,* 44, 68-82.

Helkkula, A. & Pihlström, M. (2010) Narratives and metaphors in service development. *Qualitative Market Research: An International Journal,* 13, 354-371.

Hodgkinson, G. P. & Rousseau, D. M. (2009) Bridging the Rigour–Relevance Gap in Management Research: It's Already Happening! *Journal of Management Studies,* 46, 534-546.

Ivarsson, B., Sjöberg, T. & Larsson, S. (2005) Waiting for cardiac surgery—support experienced by next of kin. *European Journal of Cardiovascular Nursing* 4, 145-152.

Kaye, B. & Jacobson, B. (1999) True Tales and Tall Tales: The Power of Organizational Storytelling. *Training & Development*, 45-50.

Kieser, A. (2011) Between rigour and relevance: Co-existing institutional logics in the field of management science. *Society and Economy,* 33, 237.

Kieser, A. & Alexander, T. N. (2005) Success Factor Research: Overcoming the Trade-Off Between Rigor and Relevance? *Journal of Management Inquiry,* 14, 275-279

Kieser, A. & Leiner, L. (2009) Why the Rigour–Relevance Gap in Management Research Is Unbridgeable. *Journal of Management Studies,* 46, 516-533.

Krueger, R. A. & Casey, M. A. (2000) *Focus groups: a practical guide for applied research,* Thousand Oaks, Calif., Sage.

Ljungberg, J. & Bergquist, M. (2005) Tales from the Crypt - Organizing IT-Business in the Dotcom era. *In:* ed. IRIS 28, Kristiansand, N., August 6-9, 2005.

Løwendahl, B. R. & Revang, Ø. (1998) Challenges to existing strategy theory in a postindustrial society. *Strategic Management Journal,* 19, 755-773.

Mayo, E. (1933) *The human problems of an industrial civilization,* New York, MacMillan.

Pettigrew, A. M. (2011) Scholarship with Impact. *British Journal of Management,* 22, 347-354.

Pettigrew, A. M., Woodman, R. W. & Cameron, K. S. (2001) Studying organizational change and development: Challenges for future research *Academy of Management Journal,* 44, , 697-713

Polit, D. F. & Beck, C. T. (2004) *Nursing research: Appraising evidence for nursing practice (7th Edition),* Philadelphia, Wolters Klower/Lippincott Williams & Wilkins.

Polzer, J. T., Gulati, R., Khurana, R. & Tushman, M. L. (2009) Crossing Boundaries to Increase Relevance in Organizational Research. *Journal of Management Inquiry,* 18, 280-286.

Pratt, M. G. (2009) For the lack of a boilerplate: Tips on writing up qualitative research. *Academy of Management Journal,* 52, 856-862.

Query, J. L. J. & Wright, K. (2003) Assessing communication competence in an online study: toward informing interventions among older adults with cancer. *Journal of Health Communication,* 15, 203-218.

Rynes, S. L., Bartunek, J. M. & Daft, R. L. (2001) Across the Great Divide: Knowledge Creation and Transfer between Practitioners and Academics. *The Academy of Management Journal,* 44, 340-355.

Siggelkow, N. (2007) Persuasion with case studies. *Academy of Management Journal,* 50, 20-24.

Silen-Lipponen, M., Tossavainen, K., Kurunen, H. & Smith, A. (2004) Learning about teamwork in operating room clinical placement. *British Journal of Nursing,* 13, 244-253.

Starkey, K. & Madan, P. (2001) Bridging the Relevance Gap: Aligning Stakeholders in the Future of Management Research. *British Journal of Management,* 12, S3-S26.

Strauss, A. & Corbin, J. (1994) Grounded Theory Methodology: An overview. *In:* Denzin, N. K. & Lincoln, Y. S. (eds.) *Handbook of Qualitative Research.* London: Sage.

Strauss, A. & Corbin, J. (1998) *Basics of qualitative research: Techniques and procedures for developing grounded theory,* Thousand Oaks, CA Sage.

Symon, G. & Cassell, C. (2004) *Essential Guide to Qualitative Methods in Organizational Research*, Sage Publications Ltd

Vermeulen, F. (2005) On Rigor and Relevance: Fostering Dialectic Progress in Management Research. *Academy of Management Journal,* 48, 978-982.

Westbrook, J. I., Coiera, E. W., Sophie Gosling, A. & Braithwaite, J. (2007) Critical incidents and journey mapping as techniques to evaluate the impact of online evidence retrieval systems on health care delivery and patient outcomes. *International journal of medical informatics,* 76, 234-245.

Yin, R. K. (1994) *Case Study Research: Design and Methods,* Thousand Oaks, Sage.

Ölvingson, C. (2002) Using the critical incident technique to define a minimal data set for requirements elicitation in public health. *International Journal of Medical Informatics,* 68, 165-174

The Critical Incident Technique as a Tool for Gathering Data as Part of a Qualitative Study of Information Seeking Behaviour

Rita Marcella, Hayley Rowlands and Graeme Baxter
Robert Gordon University, Aberdeen, UK
Originally published in ECRM (2013) Conference Proceedings

Editorial Commentary

While acknowledging the different uses to which Flanagan's (1954) Critical Incident Technique (CIT) has been inducted, Marcella, Rowlands and Baxter present an overview of how the CIT can be used in the area of information behaviour. Two areas in which such a technique can be applied are presented, namely in quantitative and qualitative studies. The inconsistencies and tensions of such applications are identified and commented upon in academic studies. The use of the CIT is applied onto a study of the behaviour of oil and gas professionals within the context of health and safety. The impact of contextual factors on the feelings of participants, its advantages and drawbacks are discussed in the light of how academics and practitioners make use of the CIT as a tool of and for research. The application of the steps needs further development.

Abstract: Since devised by Flanagan in 1954 as a tool to explore what people do to achieve an organisational aim, the critical incident technique (CIT) has been used in various disciplines as a method of understanding human behaviour. This paper provides an overview of the use of CIT in the specific field of information behaviour, both in large-scale quantitative studies designed to assess the quality and impact of library and information systems and services, and in more qualitative research examining the information needs and use of particular professions or occupational groups, or of particular societal or community groups. It highlights the inconsistent application of CIT in academic research, and the quantitative versus qualitative tension that exists in discussions of the use of CIT as a data collection tool. The paper also discusses the use of CIT by the authors in a study of the information seeking behaviour of oil and gas professionals in a health and safety context, considering that project in relation to Flanagan's five main steps in the CIT process, and in terms of the benefits and limitations of the technique identified by Flanagan and by other commentators. The authors believe that CIT has particular advantages in the study of information behaviour as a method of illuminating the ways in which the context of information need impacts on information behaviour, how participants feel, and in particular in identifying positive and negative behaviours in information seeking and use. The authors also argue that CIT must be used in a thoughtful manner and in a full recognition of its weaknesses in the design of future research.

Keywords: critical incident technique, information behaviour, qualitative techniques

1   Introduction

The critical incident technique (hereafter CIT) has its roots in the Aviation Psychology Program of the US Army Air Forces during World War II, where it was used in the selection and classification of aircrews. Almost ten years after the war, one of the psychologists involved in the programme, John C. Flanagan, wrote a now famous paper on the development of the methodology and its subsequent use in a number of studies exploring the critical requirements for specific occupational groups or activities (Flanagan 1954). In his paper, Flanagan (p.327) defined CIT as consisting of "a set of procedures for collecting direct observations of human behavior in such a way as to facilitate their potential usefulness in solving practical problems and developing broad psychological principles". For an incident to be critical, Flanagan argued (p.327), it "must occur in a situation where the purpose or intent of the act seems fairly clear to the observer and where its consequences are sufficiently definite to leave little doubt concerning its effects".

While Flanagan's paper placed a clear emphasis on data collection through the direct observation of human behaviour by trained observers, he acknowledged that, "if suitable precautions are taken, recalled incidents can be relied on to provide adequate data…" (p.340). Indeed, he was at pains to point out that the technique "does not consist of a single rigid set of rules governing such data collection. Rather it should be thought of as a flexible set of principles which must be modified and adapted to meet the

specific situation at hand" (p.335). Flanagan suggested that four procedures could be used in collecting recalled data in the form of critical incidents: individual interviews; group interviews; questionnaires; and/or "record forms" (i.e. where the participants record details of critical incidents
in narrative form, or where they place a 'check' or 'tick' in the appropriate
place on a pre-determined list of the most likely incidents to occur).

In 2005, in a paper celebrating 50 years of CIT, Butterfield et al. (2005)
championed both this flexibility and the subsequent diversity of discipli-
nary application. They noted that the technique has been utilised across a
wide range of subject areas, including counselling, education and teaching,
marketing, medicine, nursing and social work. They also concluded, however, that the CIT's flexibility has become something of a "double-edged
sword", as it has "encouraged the proliferation of approaches and termi-
nology" (p. 476). For example, they catalogue several studies in which the
data analysis procedures have diverged from those outlined by Flanagan
(Butterfield et al. 2005, p.481); and, to highlight terminological inconsistencies, they list a number of phrases used in studies adopting CIT, including 'critical event technique', 'critical incident exercise' and 'critical incident reflection' (p. 476).

This current paper discusses the use of CIT as a methodology in the domain
of library and information science (LIS), and more specifically in the field of
information behaviour. It will provide an overview of some of the published studies in this area, before focusing on a recent project, conducted
by the authors, which used CIT to explore the information seeking behaviour of oil and gas professionals in a health and safety context.

2   CIT use in information behaviour studies

As Urquhart (2001) explains, the use of the critical incident technique in
information behaviour research has tended to revolve around the examination of "a brief, but memorable information seeking episode", where
the researchers have asked participants to provide one or more examples
of occasions when they have sought information in order to, say, solve a
problem or make a decision, to discuss the methods used in acquiring the
information, and to evaluate the value and impact of the information obtained.

A number of these studies have been large-scale, questionnaire-based exercises, designed largely to assess the quality and impact of library and information systems and services. For example, Radford (2006) explored young people's perceptions of public librarians and library staff in New York City, by gathering details of both "good" and "unpleasant or bad" experiences in public libraries from over 2,400 fifth and seventh grade students. Also in New York, Small and Snyder (2009), in a study of the impact of school libraries on student achievement and motivation, used an "open-ended critical incident probe" to ask respondents to reflect on a particular event or activity in which the school library "helped or excited students about learning something new". Tenopir, meanwhile, has been part of a team that has written a series of papers on academic faculty's readership of scholarly articles (e.g. Tenopir, King and Bush, 2004; Tenopir et al., 2009; Tenopir, 2012). Here, they have used a variation of CIT, which they term the "incident of last reading", in order to both assess information-seeking and reading patterns, and demonstrate the value of libraries' journal collections. Urquhart et al. (2003, p.76) highlight the problems associated with a self-completion questionnaire approach, where "respondents...despite instructions supplied, had answered the questionnaire in general terms, giving details about what they usually did...rather than detailing what happened on one particular incident". Conversely, Serenko and Turel (2010) describe the successful use of CIT in a paper-based survey of Canadian university students' positive and negative incidents relating to email usage, citing as benefits of CIT that novel descriptions of previously unrecorded phenomena may be generated.

Of greater interest to the present authors is the use of CIT in more qualitative information behaviour studies, where the technique has been integrated into interview instruments. Of the studies discussed in the literature, several focus on particular professions or occupational groups, frequently in the healthcare professions. Indeed, Urquhart et al. (2003, pp. 72-74) provide a tabular overview of CIT studies in the health sector, conducted between 1983 and 2001. More recently, the information behaviour of health professions has been the subject of CIT-based research ranging from Musoke's 2007 study of the accessibility and use of health information among primary healthcare providers in rural Uganda, to the investigation of the information challenges facing non-clinical managers in rural Nova Scotia, Canada, by MacDonald et al. (2011). The academic community, too, has been the subject of a number of qualitative CIT studies, aided presumably by the relative convenience of research participants. These have included studies of academic staff, such as Jamali and Asadi's 2010 exploration of the role of Google in the information seeking behaviour of physicists and astronomers, and Makri and Blandford's examination, in 2012, of the ways in which interdisciplinary researchers come across information serendipitously. They have also included student-focused projects, such as the research conducted by Kerins et al. (2004) which explored the information behaviour of engineering and law students in Ireland, where the critical incident focused on their final year project.

Elsewhere, CIT has been used as the basis for interviews in a range of occupational information behaviour studies conducted internationally, from the examination of artisan fisher folk in Uganda (Ikoja-Odongo and Ocholla, 2003), to Zach's 2005 study of how senior arts administrators in the US decide when they have found "enough" information to complete management tasks. And from Lambert's 2010 study of how Southern Baptist ministers in the midwestern US obtain information for administrative or pastoral purposes, to the investigation of the ways in which Kuwaiti journalists seek information for journalistic assignments (Chaudry and Al-Sagheer, 2011).

Away from the workplace environment, a number of information behaviour researchers have used CIT within the framework of everyday life information seeking (ELIS), which Savolainen (1995, pp 266-7) defined as "the acquisition of various informational (both cognitive and expressive) elements which people employ to orient themselves in daily life or to solve problems not directly connected with the performance of occupational tasks". Some of this research has attempted to look at a broad cross-section of a particular community, including Savolainen's own study (1995) of the residents of Tampere, Finland; and Johnson's (2004) investigation of the role of social networks and social capital in the information seeking behaviour of the residents of Ulaanbaatar, Mongolia. Other studies have focused on particular societal groups, or on individuals at particular stages of the life cycle. For example, Jiyane and Ocholla (2004) studied the information needs and sources of women in a rural community in South Africa, while Hamer (2003) used CIT interviews with young gay men to acquire data on their information behaviour relating to coming out. Julien (1999) explored the barriers that Canadian adolescents face in accessing information helpful for career decision making; while Niemelä and Huotari (2008) investigated the information use of Finnish senior citizens.

While Davenport (2010), in a review of the use of three "confessional methods" in ELIS research, describes CIT as a "fitting technique for analyzing…confessional phenomena", and argues that the confessional approach is particularly apposite for ELIS, she is critical of the ways in which CIT has actually been used in the ELIS field. In particular, she notes that the number of critical incidents required for "robust analysis" is rarely achieved, that few researchers comply with Flanagan's protocols, and that his caveats are "rarely discussed, let alone heeded" (p. 539). However, this charge could equally be levelled at the use of CIT in other social science research (Butterfield et al. 2005, p.476). Urquhart et al. (2003, p. 65) are also critical of the lack of methodological detail in the published accounts of many CIT studies.

Bearing these points in mind, the following section of this paper will discuss the present authors' use of CIT to explore information behaviour in an oil and gas, health and safety context. Although it should be emphasised here that, in designing the study, the researchers did not have Flanagan's protocols in mind. Rather, they drew upon some of their previous, interview-based, information behaviour research in which participants focused on recent information-seeking incidents or episodes. For example, Marcella and Illingworth (2012) used such an approach when studying the information behaviour of UK entrepreneurs encountering business failure; while Baxter, Marcella and Illingworth (2010), in exploring organisational information behaviour during Scottish Government public consultation exercises, asked interviewees to consider the example of the most recent consultation to which they had responded. While the current authors did not, themselves, adhere rigidly to Flanagan's guidance, they will consider their research in relation to his five main steps in the CIT process, and in terms of the benefits and limitations of CIT identified by Flanagan and by other commentators.

3   The use of CIT as a tool to gather data about information behaviour in the oil and gas industry

The study which provided the basis for this paper and reflections on the use of CIT as a data collection method was conducted in 2011 and was sponsored by an engineering software provider, focusing on the oil and gas sector. The study explored the role of information systems in enhancing health, safety and emergency response in the oil and gas industry and gathered useful perspectives on the role of information systems in enhancing health and safety management. The study also uncovered insights into the information seeking behaviour of oil and gas professionals in a health and safety context. The project was particularly timely in that it took place when the critical nature of health and safety in the energy sector continued to receive considerable attention internationally, particularly following the high-profile Deepwater Horizon disaster in 2010. Indeed, a commission appointed by President Obama to investigate the Gulf of Mexico explosion and oil spill concluded that "most, if not all, of the failures at Macondo can be traced back to underlying failures of management and communication" (National Commission on the BP Deepwater Horizon Oil Spill and Offshore Drilling, 2011, p.122). The research described here coincided with that discussed in the only other known published paper on CIT-based information behaviour research in the energy sector, where Ibrahim and Allen (2012) explored the relationship between information sharing and trust during major incidents in the oil industry, interviewing 19 employees of a major multinational oil company in the process.

The present authors' study was undertaken in two distinct stages, in a mix of quantitative and qualitative approaches: 1) an online questionnaire survey of over 370 individuals in the oil and gas industry, completed largely by health and safety managers, senior managers and engineers located across the globe; and 2) a series of in-depth interviews utilising critical incidents as a focus. It is the second stage of the project which forms the basis of the discussion below, relating this to Flanagan's five key steps in the CIT process.

Understanding the general aims of the activity being studied: Flanagan (1954, p. 336) notes that a basic condition for any use of CIT is a "fundamental orientation in terms of the general aims of the activity" being studied. The main focus of this study was, of course, the role of information systems and information behaviour in enhancing health and safety in the oil and gas industry. The present authors have an extensive background in LIS research, and, through a number of other recent research projects commissioned by industry, have developed a sound knowledge of health and safety management in the energy sector. Of critical importance here, though, was the input of the commissioning company. All survey questions and interview schedules were designed in consultation with the research sponsors, to reflect industry perspectives. On reflection, while the process of collaborative research design can be challenging, with industry-led research focusing on broad lessons, and academic research focusing on the 'small detail', such an approach was felt to be an effective exercise in ensuring that the research instruments were well designed.

Making plans and setting specifications: As the second stage of the CIT process, Flanagan (1954, pp. 337-339) called for researchers to set precise plans and specifications. He urged that the types of situations to be explored – the critical incidents – should be relevant and clearly defined, and that those conducting the research should be familiar with the types of incident being studied and be consistent in their approach. In the current study, the critical incidents to be discussed in the interviews were all predetermined by the participating businesses from the oil and gas sector, with agreement from the research team. While the incidents could be chosen by the organisations, they had to meet two basic criteria: 1) that any incident be substantial enough in nature that the information aspects of dealing with the situation might be explored fully in the CIT interview; and 2) that they be significant enough to have caused potential detrimental impact to the organisation, but not sufficiently high profile to jeopardise participant anonymity. To ensure consistency of approach, the interviews were all conducted by the same member of the research team. Flanagan (1954, p. 341) also highlighted the need to "try out" questions with a small group of typical participants before being put into general use in a study. However, as Urquhart et al. (2003, p. 65) point out, many published CIT studies fail to provide any details on how, or indeed if, such piloting was conducted. In this research, to ensure the effectiveness of the interview instrument, the interviewer first conducted pilot interviews with three individuals with experience of working either in the oil and gas industry or in a health and safety role.

Collecting the data: Flanagan (1954, p. 343) noted that sample size in CIT studies is determined less by the number of participants involved, than by the number of critical incidents (and associated "critical behaviors") observed or reported, and whether or not these adequately represent the activities being studied. While he noted that "there does not appear to be a simple answer to this question", he discussed samples in terms of hundreds or thousands of incidents. Davenport (2010, p. 538), observes that these numbers are rarely met in information behaviour research, but fails to acknowledge the resource levels required to conduct CIT research on such a scale. Urquhart et al. (2003, p. 65), on the other hand, note that "few studies can afford [that] level of research effort". Certainly, in industry-sponsored projects such as that described here, researchers rarely have the luxury of the time and financial resources necessary to gather samples of that size.

The CIT element of the study discussed here was based on just four critical incidents, one identified by each of four participating companies. Enlisting organisational participants proved difficult, largely due to the subject nature of the research. Understandably, businesses were cautious about openly discussing incidents that might be considered embarrassing and commercially sensitive. This problem was, presumably, also encountered by Ibrahim and Allen (2012) in their research, as they note that they had a signed confidentiality agreement with the participating oil production company. The four businesses participating in this study were recruited via the online survey, the online professional networking site, *LinkedIn*, or via the researchers' industry contacts. The four companies consisted of an operator, a contractor, a manufacturer, and a logistics company; although this range of business types was achieved more by accident than design. The four critical incidents on which the interviews were based were, respectively:

- the 2010 Icelandic ash cloud and its effects on the safe transportation of staff between onshore and offshore installations, which was considered potentially detrimental to business performance;
- a software failure, resulting in the loss of data with health and safety implications;
- the potential contamination of thousands of pockets of private land, due to industrial and domestic fuel container leakage; and
- a chemical spillage following a traffic accident at a major city road junction.

The duration of these four events ranged from one week to around eight years, and interviews were sought from key individuals instrumental in dealing with the incidents and their aftermaths, and who were thus able to comment critically on the impact that information behaviour had had on their company's capacity to respond. Interviews were conducted with eleven individuals from across the four companies, either face-to-face or by telephone. The research team had also sought participation from employees from a range of hierarchical levels, to reflect the differing perspectives within a response team dealing with a critical incident. As a result, the interviewees occupied a variety of roles, including investigator, supervisor, lead response, safety advisor, duty manager and data analyst.

All interviewees were given advance notice of the critical incident to be discussed, although the precise nature of the interview questions was not revealed prior to the interviews taking place. As Flanagan (1954, p. 339) rightly advises, recalled critical incidents are best recorded "while the facts are still fresh in the mind". While three of the four incidents had occurred in the 12 months prior to the interviews taking place, the fourth incident (that of the fuel container leakage) had been a lengthy affair first identified in 2001, ten years before this research took place. Despite this time lapse, there was little evidence of any significant deviance between the basic accounts of the individuals involved in that incident. And while the researchers acknowledge that respondents from within particular companies, having had prior notification of the critical incident to be explored, would have had the opportunity to consult company documentation on the incident, or to discuss it with their colleagues, there was no obvious evidence of any 'collusion' having taken place in an attempt to provide consistent accounts. With one incident, the company concerned also provided a copy of their internal report on the event, further verifying their employees' verbal accounts.

All interviewees talked freely and at length about the incidents and their associated information behaviours. The researchers believe that the use of CIT gave focus to the interviews, allowing open discourse on a familiar topic, and enabling participants to describe information seeking behaviour without a need for a deep understanding or interest in the information domain on a conceptual level. Sharoff (2008) warns that participant embellishment might occur during CIT; however, the current authors feel that such embellishment will occur naturally and is not a factor which can be excluded from any study.

Analysing the data: The CIT interviews lasted between 40 and 120 minutes, were recorded with permission, and were subsequently transcribed verbatim. Flanagan describes the analysis of critical incident data as involving three distinct elements: determining a general frame of reference that will be useful for describing the critical incidents; inductively constructing a set of categories for the incidents; and deciding on the most appropriate level of specificity-generality with which to report the data. In the present study, the transcripts were analysed with recurring themes being coded in an iterative process.

Interpreting and reporting the results: Flanagan (1954, p. 345) warns that the "real errors" in CIT "are made not in the collection and analysis of the data but in the failure to interpret them properly", while both Urquhart et al. (2003) and Radford (2006) highlight the difficulty of coder interreliability. In this study, the interview transcripts were independently analysed by two members of the research team to add reliability to the interpretation of the data.

4   Conclusions

This paper has provided an overview of the use of CIT in the study of information behaviour, and has discussed its specific use in an exploration of the information seeking behaviour of oil and gas professionals in a health and safety context. It has shown that the inconsistent application of the technique has been highlighted by various observers as a weakness of CIT-based studies. However, in line with Flanagan's belief in the importance of flexibility and freedom from constraint, the current authors believe that it is the critical insight with which the study is designed that is important, and that it is only by testing research tools in an open and exploratory way that their true contribution can be evaluated. There also remains a quantitative versus qualitative tension in discussions of the use of CIT as a data collection tool. The major challenge, however, is that researchers must position their research appropriately within a research domain and not try to apply empiricist approaches to qualitative studies and vice versa. The present authors view their use of CIT as a technique in a classic qualitative tradition.

As with the use of any methodology, the CIT has strengths and weaknesses. However, the authors believe that it has particular advantages in the study of information behaviour as a method of illuminating the ways in which the context of information need impacts on information behaviour, how participants feel and in particular in identifying positive and negative behaviours in information seeking and use, which would merit further exploration. The authors would also argue that CIT must be used in a thoughtful manner and in a full recognition of its weaknesses in the design of future research. Flanagan's original conception of the CIT to better understand human behaviour in the course of achieving an aim is fundamental to information behaviour research and his design of the CIT process recognised the need for flexible evolution of the tool. It is hoped that a body of work extending this understanding of its contribution to information behaviour research will continue to evolve.

References

Baxter, G., Marcella, R. and Illingworth, L. (2010). Organisational information behaviour in the public consultation process in Scotland, Information Research, Vol. 15, No. 4, http://informationr.net/ir/15-4/paper442.html

Butterfield, L. D., Borgen, W. A., Amundson, N. E. and Maglio, A. T. (2005) "Fifty years of the critical incident technique: 1954-2004 and beyond", Qualitative Research, Vol. 5, No. 4, November, pp 475-497.

Chaudry, A. S. and Al-Sagheer, L. (2011) "Information behavior of journalists: analysis of critical incidents of information finding and use", The International Information & Library Review, Vol. 43, No. 4, pp 178-183.

Davenport, E. (2010) "Confessional methods and everyday life information seeking", Annual Review of Information Science and Technology, Vol. 44, No. 1, pp 533-562.

Flanagan, J. C. (1954) "The critical incident technique", Psychological Bulletin, Vol. 51, No. 4, July, pp 327-358.

Hamer, J. S. (2003) "Coming-out: gay males' information seeking", School Libraries Worldwide, Vol. 9, No. 2, pp 73-89.

Ibrahim, N. H. and Allen, D. (2012) "Information sharing and trust during major incidents: findings from the oil industry", Journal of the American Society for Information Science and Technology, Vol. 63, No. 10, pp 1916-1928.

Ikoja-Odongo, R. and Ocholla, D. N. (2003) "Information needs and information-seeking behavior of artisan fisher folk of Uganda", Library & Information Science Research, Vol. 25, No. 1, pp 89-105.

Jamali, H. R. and Asadi, S. (2010) "Google and the scholar: the role of Google in scientists' information-seeking behaviour", Online Information Review, Vol. 34, No. 2, pp 282-294.

Jiyane, V. and Ocholla, D. N. (2004) "An exploratory study of information availability and exploitation by the rural women of Melmoth, KwaZulu-Natal", South African Journal of Libraries & Information Science, Vol. 70, No. 1, pp 1-9.

Johnson, C. A. (2004) "Choosing people: the role of social capital in information seeking behaviour", Information Research, Vol. 10, No. 1, http://informationr.net/ir/10-1/paper201.html

Julien, H. E. (1999) "Barriers to adolescents' information seeking for career decision making", Journal of the American Society for Information Science, Vol. 50, No. 1, pp 38-48.

Kerins, G., Madden, R. and Fulton, C. (2004). "Information seeking and students studying for professional careers: the cases of engineering and law students in Ireland", Information Research, Vol. 10, No. 1, http://informationr.net/ir/10-1/paper208.html

Lambert, J. D. (2010) "The information-seeking habits of Baptist ministers", Journal of Religious & Theological Information, Vol. 9, No. 1-2, pp 1-19.

MacDonald, J., Bath, P. and Booth, A. (2011) "Information overload and information poverty: challenges for healthcare services managers?", Journal of Documentation, Vol. 67, No. 2, pp 238-263.

Makri, S. and Blandford, A. (2012) "Coming across information serendipitously – part 1: a process model", Journal of Documentation, Vol. 68, No. 5, pp 684-705.

Marcella, R. and Illingworth, L. (2012) "The impact of information behaviour on small business failure", Information Research, Vol. 17, No. 3, http://informationr.net/ir/17-3/paper525.html

Musoke, M. G. N. (2007) "Information behaviour of primary health care providers in rural Uganda", Journal of Documentation, Vol. 63, No. 3, pp 299-322.

National Commission on the BP Deepwater Horizon Oil Spill and Offshore Drilling (2011). Deep water: the Gulf oil disaster and the future of offshore drilling, http://www.oilspillcommission.gov/final-report

Niemelä, R. and Huotari, M. (2008) "Information use and enactment: the perspective of senior citizens' everyday life information behavior", Paper read at the International Conference for the Celebration of the 20th Anniversary of Information Studies, Oulu, Finland, 23-25 June.

Radford, M. L. (2006) "The critical incident technique and the qualitative evaluation of the Connecting Libraries and Schools Project", Library Trends, Vol. 55, No. 1, pp 46-64.

Savolainen, R. (1995) "Everyday life information seeking: approaching information seeking in the context of "way of life", Library & Information Science Research, Vol. 17, No. 3, pp 259-294.

Serenko, A. and Turel, O. (2010) "Rigor and relevance: the application of the critical incident technique to investigate email usage", Journal of Organizational Computing and Electronic Commerce, Vol. 20, No. 2, pp 182-207.

Sharoff, L. (2008). "Critique of the critical incident technique", Journal of Research in Nursing, Vol. 14, No. 4, pp 301-309.

Small, R. V. and Snyder, J. (2009) "The impact of New York's school libraries on student achievement and motivation: phase II—in-depth study. School Library Media Research, Vol. 12, http://www.ala.org/aasl/aaslpubsandjournals/slmrb/slmrcontents/volume12/small_phase2

Tenopir, C. (2012) "Beyond usage: measuring library outcomes and value", Library Management, Vol. 33, No. 1/2, pp 5-13.

Tenopir, C., King, D. W. and Bush, A. (2004) "Medical faculty's use of print and electronic journals: changes over time and in comparison with scientists", Journal of the Medical Library Association, Vol. 92, No. 2, pp 233-241.

Tenopir, C., King, D. W., Edwards, S. and Wu, L. (2009) "Electronic journals and changes in scholarly article seeking and reading patterns", Aslib Proceedings, Vol. 61, No. 1, pp 5-32.

Urquhart, C. (2001) "Bridging information requirements and information needs assessment: do scenarios and vignettes provide a link?", Information Research, Vol. 6, No. 2, http://informationr.net/ir/6-2/paper102.html

Urquhart, C., Light, A., Thomas, R., Barker, A., Yeoman, A., Cooper, J., Armstrong, C., Fenton, R., Lonsdale, R. and Spink, S. (2003) "Critical incident technique and explicitation interviewing in studies of information behavior", Library & Information Science Research, Vol. 25, No. (1), pp 63-88.

Zach, L. (2005) "When is "enough" enough? Modelling the information-seeking and stopping behavior of senior arts administrators", Journal of the American Society for Information Science and Technology, Vol. 56, No. 1, pp 23-35.

Application of Cluster Analysis and Discriminant Analysis in Market Segmentation and Prediction

Ruth Yeung[1] and Wallace Yee[2]
[1]Institute for Tourism Studies, Macao, China
[2]Faculty of Business Administration, University of Macau, Macao, China
Originally published in ECRM (2012) Conference Proceedings

Editorial Commentary

This paper addresses the question as to whether the use of cluster analysis and discriminant analysis may be used in tandem to better segment a market. Specifically, the authors discuss the growing market between Mainland China and the Pearl River Delta regions. By combining the two methodologies in their data analysis, the authors are able to determine three distinct market segments within this shopping group and to further determine the motivations and attitudes of the individuals within the groups. Further, the authors take the reader through numerous analytical steps to better demonstrate how cluster analysis may be used with discriminant analysis to achieve segmentation of a specific marking, thus providing extremely valuable insight into the consumer characteristics for the entities doing business, or contemplating opening a business in a location frequented by tourist shoppers.

Abstract: Cluster analysis is commonly used for classifying subjects, but the analytical technique often receives skepticisms of the way of measuring of similarity and the number of clusters. Despite applying discriminant analysis can improve target segmentation accuracy; this analytical technique is less adopted. Hence, the underlying purpose of this paper is to demonstrate how cluster analysis in conjunction with discriminant analysis can be applied in a multifaceted business field in tourism research as targeting an optimal market segments is crucial to organization success.

With the growth of cross border shopping between the Pearl River Delta Regions in Greater China after the launch of "one year multiple endorsements" of the Individual Visit Scheme by the Chinese government, many popular international brands start to set up shops in Hong Kong and Macau to capture the emerging market. As such, this study adopted hierarchical cluster analysis, followed by K means cluster analysis to classify cross border shoppers into mutually exclusive groups based on their motivation and attitudes in the context. Cross tabulation analysis was then conducted to test if there is any association between the product/service purchased and the cluster membership of respondents. Finally, discriminant analysis was employed to assess the adequacy of classification, and to determine which variables are the best predictors of group membership so that the variables can be used to predict new cases of group membership in the context. To achieve the research purpose, quantitative research design was adopted and data was collected using intercept method with convenience sampling technique. A total of 194 respondents who normally reside in Mainland China were recruited, and their motivation and attitudes on cross-border shopping in Hong Kong were measured. Results of the cluster analysis suggest that there exist three distinct groups of cross-border shoppers based on the motivational and attitudinal criteria. The attitudes towards product price and quality, agglomeration of comprehensive retails, together with age, marital status, education, occupation, types of goods purchased, and frequency of visit are significantly different among the three groups. The cross tabulation analysis reveals that there was an association between cluster membership of respondents and purchase of high involvement products such as photographic equipment, and certain food products. Using discriminant analysis, the group membership of tourists was predicted based on their experience such as comfortable shopping environment, salesperson's product knowledge, easy to cross-border and convenient opening hours; and the product attributes such as product price and quality, and comprehensive agglomeration of retails. This research provides a quantitative basis for formulating marketing plan and helps the industry to reduce the uncertainty in the decision making process and increase the probability of success through a systematic and objective analysis. The practical information can be translatable into operational scheme in terms of targeting, and cross-border shopping can be promoted in a strategic approach.

Keywords: customers classification, group membership, cross border shopping, motivation, attitudes

1   Introduction

Market segmentation has become a frequently used strategic marketing tool as it helps to break the entire market into a series of smaller markets according to consumer characteristics. To be effective, market segmentation cannot be based on a single factor; so, homogenous clusters should be formed with a combination of variables. Cluster analysis serves this purpose well for classifying a sample of subjects / objects on the basis of a set of measured variables into a number of different groups with similar subjects / objects placing in the same group (Cornish, 2007). The purpose of cluster analysis is indeed to classify entities into mutually exclusive and collectively exhaustive groups with homogeneity within clusters but heterogeneity among clusters. So, cluster analysis is treated as a common technique for market segmentation which can be used to identify groups of entities such as people, markets or organizations; in looking for a better understanding of purchase behaviors by identifying homogeneous groups of consumers; serves as an alternative to factor analysis and discriminant analysis; utilized to test market selection or conducted as a general data reduction tool (Punj and Stewart, 1983). Though cluster analysis is commonly used for classifying subjects, the analytical technique often receives skepticisms of the way of measuring of similarity and the number of clusters.

To overcome this discrepancy, discriminant analysis can be employed to improve the accuracy of target segmentation for discriminant analysis is a statistical technique to correctly categorizing observations or entities into homogeneous groups. It can serve the descriptive purpose to assess the adequacy of classification or the predictive one to assign entities to one of the groups of entities. However, this analytical technique is less likely to be adopted. The possible reason for this, to the best of our knowledge, most literature appears to focus more on the theoretical foundation of these two statistical analyses with litter guidance on how to carrying out the technique for marketing research as well as how these two techniques could complement each other in market segmentation and prediction.

Hence, this paper aims to demonstrate how cluster analysis in conjunction with discriminant analysis can be applied in a multifaceted business field in tourism research as targeting an optimal market segments is crucial to organization success. This study uses Mainland Chinese cross border shoppers across the Pearl River Delta regions as the context. The first reason for choosing this context is due to the enormous market potential of Chinese population and the rapid economic growth has stimulated Chinese outbound travel and spending. Secondly, cross border shopping becomes a trend under the "one year multiple endorsements" of the Individual Visit Scheme which allows many Mainland Chinese cross border to Hong Kong or Macau for shopping and consumption as these cities top their first-choice destinations list. With over 1.3 billion population, it can be understood that heterogeneity would exist among people in Mainland China. With the growth of cross border shopping in the Greater Pearl River Delta Regions, many popular international brands start to set up shops in Hong Kong and Macau to capture the emerging market. A better understanding of the characteristics and shopping habits of cross border shoppers can help to predict and target potential consumers for future business.

2   Characteristics of cross border shoppers

Different international market environments and the challenge of moving goods across border make cross border shopping more complex than domestic shopping (Piron, 2001). The extant literature states that tourists' shopping behaviour tends to differ from usual habit when they shop at home town (Stansfield, 1971). Hence, demographic characteristics that generally used as the basis for segmenting the domestic market may not be sufficient to categorize cross border segments. Moreover, using macro-economic and political criteria for segmentation may overlook the within-country heterogeneity of cross border shoppers (Hofstede, et al., 1999).

Miller (2001) suggests that there exists a link between attitudinal criteria and consumer motivations for shopping across border. A number of researchers comment that the main motivation for cross border shopping builds on the economic advantage of product price, perceived product quality, variety of product selections, store facilities, and service provided by salesperson in the cross border region (e.g.Evans et al., 1992; Blakney and Sekely, 1994; Wang, 2004; Lau, Sin and Chan, 2005; Ghaddar and Brown, 2005; Asplund et al., 2007; Yeung and Yee, 2011). Other studies have identified a range of attributes which include attitudinal criteria, such as attractiveness of the shopping areas, convenience accessibility, product assortment and service provided by salesperson, and socioeconomic characteristics, such as age, income, education, and occupation in market segmentation of out-shoppers (e.g. Papadopoulos, 1980; Chatterjee, 1991; Piron, 2002). The set of criteria have been tested in the study of market segments of domestic shoppers against cross border shoppers in Europe (Dmitrovic and Vida, 2007).

Moreover, the types of goods purchased by tourists varied (Timothy and Butler, 1995; Di Matteo and Di Matteo, 1996; Wang, 2004, Yang, 2006) and a relationship between behaviour and the environmental setting for shopping tourism is found due to differences in goods, a wide range of specialized and traditional goods, such as tea, dairy products, cloths, leather goods, electronic goods, jewelry and so forth, and the distinguishing feature of the shopping area as well as differences in opening hours. These environmental setting provides a unique leisure and shopping experience for tourists (Jansen-Verbeke, 1991; Lord et al., 2002). The freedom to cross the border, contrast between home and neighbouring markets, as well as the awareness of purchase opportunities also contribute to the willingness to shop cross border (Lord, Putrevu and Shi, 2008; Pico, 2009; Leal, Lopez-laborda and Rodrigo, 2010).

3 Development of segmentation model

The research adapted a quantitative approach using cluster analysis to segment the tourists according to their motivation and attitudes towards cross border shopping and subsequently used discriminant analysis to predict visitors' group membership based on their motivation and attitudes.

3.1 Questionnaire design

As cluster analysis has no mechanism for differentiating between relevant and irrelevant variables, the choice of variables must be underpinned by conceptual considerations (Cornish, 2007). Hence, measures chosen for this study should represent tourists' motivation to shop across border that is relevant to the environmental factors exhibited in the Pearl River Delta regions. Focusing on opinion on cross border shopping in Hong Kong from people residing in Mainland China, a questionnaire with a set of ten variables using 7-points scales were developed following a review of extant literature (e.g. Papadopoulos, 1980; Jansen-Verbeke, 1991; Evans et al., 1992; Wang, 2004; Yang, 2006; Dmitrovic and Vida, 2007; Asplund et al., 2007; Dmitrovic and Vida, 2007; Lord, Putrevu and Shi, 2008) (Appendix).

3.2 Data collection

In order to achieve the research aim, an intercept survey was carried out in various tourist spots at different time of the day and different days of the week to minimize the over-representation of the personal characteristics of respondents (Casley and Kumar, 1992). The survey was conducted by trained interviewers who fully understood the issues relating to the survey. Respondents were requested to answer a self-administered questionnaire which was pre-tested to assure its functionality. A total of 194 usable questionnaires were collected, of which, 80 were male, 128 from 21 to 40 years of age, 109 were single, 72 were white-collar, 45 were students and 129 with an annual income below HKD8,000. Majority of respondents (74.7%) shopped across the border to Hong Kong from Mainland China for less than once per two month in average in the past year.

3.3   Identify the number of clusters - hierarchical cluster analysis

Hierarchical cluster analysis was first performed to identify the number of segments that were relatively homogeneous in the importance they at-tached to the ten motivational/attitudinal variables. The technique used an algorithm that starts with each case in a separate cluster and combines clusters until only one is left. Proximities procedure was used to generate similarity measures. The between groups linkage out of the alternatives was selected so that an observation was joined to a cluster if it has a simi-larity with at least one of the members of that cluster. Base on the coeffi-cients column (indicating the distance between the two cases or clusters joined at each stage) of the agglomeration schedule which displays the cases or clusters combined at each stage, the number of cluster was set if there exists a sudden jump in the distance coefficient when read down the column. As shown in Table 1, the sudden jump occurred at stage 191 indi-cating that it was the optimal stopping point for merging clusters and sug-gesting three clusters.

Table 1: Agglomeration schedule

Stage	Cluster Combined		Coefficients	Stage Cluster First Appears		Next Stage
	Cluster 1	Cluster 2		Cluster 1	Cluster 2	
1	31	35	.000	0	0	13
2	16	34	.000	0	0	3
3	11	16	.000	0	2	28
.						
.						
.						
187	1	72	60.570	186	176	190
188	155	192	61.000	0	180	193
189	55	166	64.667	185	182	190
190	1	55	68.989	187	189	191
191	1	117	77.534	190	0	192
192	1	136	80.158	191	0	193
193	1	155	93.567	192	188	0

3.4 Identify the cluster membership - K-mean cluster analysis

K-means cluster analysis was then conducted to identify the cluster membership by setting the number of clusters to three which was obtained from the hierarchical cluster analysis. By specifying the number of clusters equals three, the Euclidean distances between Final Cluster Centers shows that the distance between cluster 1 and cluster 2, cluster 1 and cluster 3, and cluster 2 and cluster 3 were 3.843, 3.883 and 4.361 respectively (minimum F statistic = 15.05; d.f. = 2, 194, p-value < 0.001) indicating that the clusters were significantly different from each other (Kaufman and Rousseeuw, 1990; Gong and Richman, 1995). The result reveals that the group size of the three segments were 55 respondents (27.9% of total), 80 (40.6%) and 62 (31.5%) for Group 1, Group 2 and Group 3 respectively.

3.5 Comparison of motivation and attitudes among the clusters – ANOVA analysis

The mean of total and individual groups, as well as standard deviations for the independent variables were calculated. The result of one-sample t-test with test value of 4 shows that respondents have motivation and positive attitudes towards cross border shopping except "there are bargain hunting opportunities in Hong Kong" with a mean score of 3.54 (t-value = 4.893, p-value < 0.001) (Table 2).

Table 2: Mean of motivation and attitudes towards cross border shopping

	Total				Group 1		Group 2		Group 3	
	Mean	S. D.	t-value*	p-value*	Mean	S. D.	Mean	S. D.	Mean	S. D.
Price	4.55	1.712	12.619	.000	5.04	1.440	3.20	1.441	5.59	1.214
Quality	5.51	1.256	27.779	.000	6.37	.714	4.71	1.177	5.45	1.202
Variety	4.25	1.667	10.425	.000	5.34	1.601	3.68	1.118	3.66	1.671
Service	4.98	1.388	19.860	.000	5.94	1.057	4.91	1.040	3.95	1.330
Comfortable	5.01	1.238	22.611	.000	5.94	.967	4.86	.862	4.12	1.171
Opening hours	4.78	1.375	18.066	.000	5.48	1.223	4.83	1.124	3.93	1.362
Bargain hunting	3.54	1.541	4.893	.000	4.09	1.545	3.51	1.491	2.95	1.382
Custom procedure	4.92	1.545	17.287	.000	5.82	1.278	5.07	1.276	3.69	1.314
Trend	4.29	1.560	11.504	.000	4.75	1.700	4.10	1.395	3.98	1.481
Agglomeration	5.14	1.335	22.373	.000	5.99	.945	4.55	1.243	4.88	1.352

*Test value = 4

A one-way analysis of variance (ANOVA) was employed to compare visitors' motivation and attitudes towards cross border shopping among the three segments. As shown in Table 3, price is the most important factor attributable to different clusters (mean square = 170.13), followed by service, variety, comfortable etc. Similarly, large F ratios indicate variables that are important for separating clusters (F ratio of Price = 143.957, d.f. = 2, 191). However, the K-means clustering algorithm is designed to minimize within-cluster variability; the F statistics cannot be interpreted as in a traditional ANOVA. So, the significance value reported is not a reliable estimate of the probability associated with the hypothesis of no effect for a particular variable. In other words, the F tests should be used just for descriptive purposes because the clusters have been chosen to maximize the differences among cases in different clusters only.

Table 3: Comparison of attitudes towards cross border shopping among the three clusters

	Cluster		Error		F	p-value
	Mean Square	df	Mean Square	df		
Price	170.130	2	1.182	191	143.957	.000
Service	68.129	2	1.234	191	55.219	.000
Variety	61.879	2	2.159	191	28.661	.000
Comfortable	54.352	2	.980	191	55.433	.000
Quality	44.846	2	1.125	191	39.876	.000
Opening hours	42.894	2	1.461	191	29.352	.000
Agglomeration	39.682	2	1.385	191	28.645	.000
Custom procedure	19.944	2	2.203	191	9.053	.000
Bargain hunting	18.231	2	2.208	191	8.257	.000
Trend	9.614	2	2.359	191	4.075	.018

3.6 Association between products purchased and cluster membership - cross tabulation analysis

Cross tabulation analysis was conducted to test if there is any association between the product/service purchased and the cluster membership of the three segments. Cramer's V which is a measure of association based on chi-square was calculated. The results obtained from the cross tabulation analysis reveal that there was an association between purchase of Photographic Goods, Audio-Visual Equipment, Electronic Products, Food products/Dairy products, and tea and cluster membership of respondents (Nominal by Nominal Cramer's V = 0.017, 0.017, 0.046, 0.041 and 0.025 respectively). Each of the three segments was then labeled as leisure buyers (Group 1), planned buyers (Group 2) and infrequent buyers (Group 3) according to their purchase pattern.

The characteristics and the purchase pattern of the group members were compared and summarized in Table 4.

Table 4: Characteristics and purchase pattern of the three segments

Group	Motivation and attitude	Demographic	Visit Frequency	Product purchase	Group Size
1 leisure buyers	usually scored high in every aspect of motivation and attitudes except "low product price in Hong Kong is low".	relatively young < 30 years (68.6%), mostly single (65.7%), an undergraduate degree (55.2%), Income $8,000-15,000 (23.9%)	once a week	leather goods (8%*) photographic goods (11%*) audiovisual equipment (8%*) jewelry/watch (11%)	67 samples (34.5%)
2 planned buyers	scored in-between the other groups except lowest in "Product price in Hong Kong is low", "Quality" and "Agglomeration".	relatively older > 40 years (23.2%), married /with children (29%), income < $8,000 (71%) laborer (28.9%).	twice per months	personal care products (6%*) food and/or dairy products (12%*), tea (4%*)	69 samples (35.6%)
3 infrequent buyers	scored low except highest in "Product price in Hong Kong is low"; "Quality" and "Agglomeration" in-between	mostly young adults between 21 and 40 (67.2%), highly educated with postgraduate degree (17.2%), relatively high income level >$15,000 (13.9%)	< once per two months	Books/Magazines (22.4%*) Medicine/Chinese Herbal Medicines (31%*) Beauty services / Spa (13.8%*)	58 samples (29.9%)

* Above the average percentage

4 Development of prediction model

4.1 Association between the three segments and the discriminant functions - discriminant analysis

For the discriminant analysis, the group membership, i.e. leisure buyers (Group 1), planned buyers (Group 2) and infrequent buyers (Group 3) was treated as dependent variable and the observed characteristics – motivational/attitudinal variables were treated as predictor variables. Prior to carrying out the analysis, the sampling distribution of any linear combination of the independent variables was checked for normality and absence of multicollinearity and singularity. Discriminant analysis was then performed in order to build a predictive model of group membership based on the observed characteristics of cross border shopping. The procedure generates a set of discriminant functions based on linear combinations of the predictor variables that provide the best discrimination between the segments (Tabacknick and Fidell, 2007).

4.2 Canonical discriminant functions

The two significant Canonical discriminant functions, namely "cross border shopping experience" and "product offering" obtained were significantly differed from each other at 5% level (p-value < 0.001). Furthermore, the Canonical variables "cross border shopping experience" and "product offering" accounted for 64.8% and 35.2% of the between group (explained) variance respectively.

4.3 Test of group mean difference – Wilks' lambda

The difference between the mean of the functions were tested using Wilks' lambda, the proportion of the total variance in the discriminant scores not explained by differences among the groups. Wilks' lambda obtained for the functions was 0.143 (p-value < 0.001) indicating the group means were different.

4.4 Prediction of group membership for new cases

The correlation (loading) between the variables and the discriminant function was shown in the structure matrix which indicates the usefulness of each variable in the discriminant function (Table 5). For each variable, an asterisk marks its largest absolute correlation with one of the canonical functions. By convention, loading in excess of 0.33 (i.e. 10% of variance) is considered as eligible. As shown in Table 5, "The shopping environment in

Hong Kong is comfortable" has the strongest correlation (0.490) with Function 1"cross border shopping experience", while "Product price in Hong Kong is low" has the strongest correlation (0.662) with Function 2 "product offering".

To predict the membership of new cases of cross border shopper, their motivational and attitudinal scores were fed into the three classification functions (Table 5) to obtain the classification scores using Equation 1 shown below.

Classification score of Group i = Constant for Group i + $\sum$Coefficients of Xij * Sij (Equation 1)

Where i ranges from 1 to 3,
        j ranges from 1 to 10,
        Xij denotes Variable Xj (i.e. Comfortable, Service,..., Agglomeration) of Group i, and
        Sij denotes the score of the respective Variable Xj of Group i

Group membership of the new cross border shopper was then assigned based on the highest classification score calculated.

Table 5: Structure matrix and classification function coefficients

	Structure matrix		Classification Function Coefficients		
	Function1	Func-tion2	Group 1	Group 2	Group 3
CROSS BORDER SHOPPING EX-PERIENCE					
Comfortable	.490(*)	.148	2.964	2.752	1.399
Service	.473(*)	.080	2.534	2.357	1.213
Custom procedure	.453(*)	-.044	5.113	4.356	3.218
Opening hours	.342(*)	.005	1.672	1.610	1.046
Variety	.300(*)	.290	3.461	2.537	2.320
Bargain hunting	.209(*)	.033	2.754	2.285	1.973
Trend	.132(*)	.095	1.393	1.320	1.119
PRODUCT OF-FERING					
Price	-.138	.662(*)	2.448	1.427	2.949
Quality	.216	.539(*)	2.999	1.830	3.311
Agglomeration	.238	.364(*)	1.880	1.157	1.909
Constant			-76.431	-49.115	-45.661

*The largest absolute correlation with one of the canonical functions and ordered by absolute size of correlation within function.

5   Discussion and conclusion

This study achieves the aim to demonstrate how cluster analysis in conjunction with discriminant analysis can be applied. Using cross border shopping as illustration, the study of 194 Chinese conducted cross border shopping to Hong Kong exhibits that cluster and discriminant analyses using the ten relative important shopper attitudes towards cross border shopping as clustering variables can be effectively applied to the segmentation of cross border tourism markets. The step by step procedure presents how the three distinct homogeneous segments were identified, with each segment possessing a unique group profile on the basis of the two discriminant functions, namely "cross border shopping experience" and "product offering".

Results of cluster analysis show that the attitudes towards product price and quality, agglomeration of comprehensive retails, together with age, marital status, education, occupation, types of goods purchased and frequency of visit are significantly different among the three groups. The cross tabulation analysis reveals that there was an association between cluster membership of respondents and purchase of high involvement products such as photographic equipment, and certain food products. Group 1 tends to enjoy the cross border shopping experience and views it as a leisure activity. Group 2 has indifferent view on both cross border shopping experience and the product offerings while Group 3 is likely to be concerned about the product offerings and considers shopping for essential goods and views it as a laborious activity. The group membership of tourists was predicted based on their experience such as comfortable shopping environment, salesperson's product knowledge, easy to cross-border and convenient opening hours; and the product offering such as product price and quality, and comprehensive agglomeration of retails.

The main advantage of complementary use of cluster analysis and discriminant analysis is that a predictive model of group membership could be developed through a set of discriminant functions which were derived by linking the cluster group membership with the motivational /attitudinal variables. These motivational / attitudinal profiles were meaningful and distinctive enough to offer the cross border shopping tourism marketer actionable and practical information which can be translatable into operational scheme in terms of targeting and promoting cross border shopping in a strategic approach.

Though with small sample size and non-randomly recruited sample, the study testifies that both cluster and discriminant analysis are invaluable and effective analytical techniques to profiling cross border shoppers segments in such a way that the importance of tourism destination shopping environment could be attributed to specific motivational / attitudinal orientation. The structure matrix and classification function coefficients provide an algorithm to assigning membership for new cases of cross border shopper. The application of the two analytical techniques can be extended to other study contexts and sectors.

Appendix 1

Variable	Explanation
Price	Product price in Hong Kong is low
Quality	Product bought from Hong Kong with high quality
Variety	Products / services in Hong Kong are not available in home town
Service	Hong Kong sales people provide good services
Comfortable	The shopping environment in Hong Kong is comfortable
Opening hours	Opening hours of the shops at Hong Kong are convenient
Bargain hunting	There are bargain hunting opportunities in Hong Kong
Custom procedure	Border crossing procedures to Hong Kong is simple
Trend	Follow the current trend in travelling to Hong Kong for cross border shopping
Agglomeration	Agglomeration of comprehensive retails in Hong Kong

References

Asplund, M., Friberg, R. and Wilander, F. (2007), Demand and distance: Evidence on cross border shopping, Journal of Public Economics, Vol. 91 pp.141–157.

Blakney, V. and Sekely, W. (1994), Retail attributes: influence on shopping mode behaviour, Journal of Managerial, Vol. 6 No. 1, pp. 101–118.

Chatterjee, A. (1991), "Cross border shopping: searching for a solution", Canadian Business Review, Vol. 18 No. 4, pp. 26-9.

Cornish, R. (2007), Statistics: Cluster Analysis, Mathematics Learning Support Centre.

Di Matteo, L. & Di Matteo, R. (1996), An analysis of Canadian cross border travel, Annals of Tourism Research, Vol. 23 No. 1, pp. 103-122.

Dmitrovic, T. and Vida, I. (2007), An examination of cross border shopping behaviour in South-East Europe, European Journal of Marketing, Vol. 41 No. 3, pp. 382-95.

Evans, W., Lane, H. W., O'Grady, S. and Hildebrand, T. (1992), Border crossings: doing business in the US, Scarborough, Ont: Prentice-Hall, Canada.

Fitzgerald, J., Quinn, T. P., Whelan, B. J. and Williams, J. A. (1988), An Analysis of Cross border Shopping, The Economic and Social Research Institute, Dublin.

Ghaddar, S. and Brown, C. (2005), The cross border Mexican shopper: a profile, Research Review, Vol. 12 No. 2, pp.46–50.

Gong, X. and Richman, M. B. (1995), On the Application of Cluster Analysis to Growing Season Precipitation Data in North America East of the Rockies. Journal of Climate, Vol. 8, No. 4, pp. 897-931.

Helsen, K., Jedidi, K. and Desarbo, W.S. (1993), A new approach to country segmentation utilizing multinational diffusion patterns, Journal of Marketing, Vol. 57 No. 4, pp. 1-17.

HKTB, (2011), 2010 Total tourism spending reaches all-time high of over hk$200 billion - Tourism Expenditure Associated to Inbound Tourism, Hong Kong Tourism Board, 3 April, 2011 available at http://tw.partnernet.hktb.com/pnweb/jsp/doc/listDoc.jsp?doc_id=137260 (accessed on 6/1/11)

Hofstede, F., Steenkamp, J. E. M. and Wedel, M. (1999), International market segmentation based on consumer-product relations, Journal of Marketing Research, Vol. 36 No. 1, pp. 1-17.

Jansen-Verbeke, M. (1991), Leisure shopping: a magic concept for the tourism industry. Tourism Management, 12, 9–14.

Kaufman, L. and Rousseeuw, P. J. (1990), Finding groups in data: an introduction to cluster analysis, Wiley Online Library.

Lau, H., Leo, Y., Sin, L. Y. and Chan, K. K. (2005), Chinese Cross Border Shopping: An Empirical Study, Journal of Hospitality & Tourism Research, Vol. 29, pp. 110-133.

Leal, A., Julio López-Laborda, J. and Rodrigo, F. (2010), Cross Border Shopping: A Survey, Int Adv Econ Res, Vol. 16, pp. 135–148.

Lord, K. R., Putrevu, S. and Shi. Y. Z. (2008), Cultural influences on cross border vacationing, Journal of Business Research, Vol. 61, pp. 183–190.

Mares, N. (1990), Impacts of the single European market on the spatial structure of the Netherlands and the relation between the Netherlands and the Federal Republic of Germany, Institut f .ur Raumplanung Universit.at, Dortmund.

Miller, N.J. (2001), Contributions of social capital theory in predicting rural community in-shopping behaviour, The Journal of Socio-Economics, Vol. 30, pp. 475-93.

Papadopoulos, N.G. and Heslop, L.A. (1993), Product Country Images: Impact and Their Role in International Marketing, International Business Press, New York, NY.

Papadopoulos, N.G. (1980), Consumer out-shopping research: review and extension, Journal of Retailing, Vol. 56 Winter, pp. 41-58.

Picó, M. B. (2009), Shoppers without borders: cross border shopping is big business around the world, Retailing Today, December, 2009, pp. 15-16.

Piron, F. (2001), "International retail leakages: Singaporeans outshopping in Malaysia", Singapore Management Review, Vol. 23 No. 1, pp. 35-58.

Piron, F. (2002), International outshopping and ethnocentrism, European Journal of Marketing, Vol. 36 No 1/2, pp. 189-210.

Sethi, V. and King, W. R. (1994), Development of measures to assess the extent to which an information technology application provides competitive advantage, Management Science, Vol. 40 No. 12, pp. 1601-27.

Stansfield, C. A. (1971), The Nature of Seafront Development and Social Status of Seaside Resorts, Society and Leisure, Vol. 4, pp.117-141.

Tabachnick B G & Fidell L S (2007), Using Multivariate Statistics, Harper & Row, Publishers, Inc, New York.

Timothy, D. J., & Butler, R. W. (1995), Cross border shopping: a North American perspective, Annals of Tourism Research, Vol. 22 No. 1, pp. 16–34.

Wang, D. (2004), Hong Kongers' cross border consumption and shopping in Shenzhen: patterns and motivations, Journal of Retailing and Consumer Services, Vol. 11, pp. 149–159.

Yang, C. (2006), The Pearl River Delta and Hong Kong: an evolving cross-boundary region under ''one country, two systems'', Habitat International, Vol. 30, pp. 61–86.

Yeung, R. M. W. and Yee, W. M. S. (2011), "Cross border shopping: stimulant factors for crossing from China to Macao". Proceedings of the Academy of Marketing Conference 2011: Marketing Field Forever, 5-7 July, Academy of Marketing, Liverpool, UK.

Student Satisfaction Formation: Linkage Between Information Satisfaction and College Choice Satisfaction

Nurlida Ismail[1], Faridah Hj Hassan[2] and Nooraini Mohamad Sheriff[2]
[1]Taylor's University, Subang Jaya, Malaysia
[2]Universiti Teknologi MARA, Shah Alam, Malaysia
Originally published in ECRM (2012) Conference Proceedings

Editorial Commentary

The paper discusses the importance of proper marketing techniques by a university to prospective students by using sufficient information to create student satisfaction. This presents an interesting concept by portraying the university as a business entity and the student as a consumer. The authors developed a model for the study which incorporates three constructs, college attributes, accessibility, information satisfaction and college choice satisfaction. A comprehensive table including various conceptual definitions is also provided. The authors proceeded to run Structural Equation Modelling to the data collected from the 620 viable surveys. The authors further discuss the importance of information on college attributes, the accessibility of the information, and the level of student choice satisfaction; the most important indicates of each are also shared. This is a very interesting study and it would be of further interest to perhaps determine the length of time the subjects had attended the university. In other words, are the students still in the honeymoon phase of their attendance at the university, or are they still satisfied with their choice of university after attending for a specific length of time?

Nurlida Ismail, Faridah Hj Hassan & Nooraini Mohamad Sheriff

Abstract: Satisfaction level that students have in their college choice can have a long term impact on the continued existence of the college. Hence, student satisfaction is considered an important performance indicator. This study investigates the relationship between information characteristics (comprises of information on college attributes and information accessibility), information satisfaction and college choice satisfaction. Structured questionnaire was employed and self- administered survey approach was used to gather data. Two types of analysis were presented. Firstly, descriptive statistics was employed to describe the basic features of the data for each item in a construct. While the second analyses involved the establishment of the measurement model as well as testing the model fit for each construct using structural equation modeling (SEM). The findings of this study provided a very interesting discovery. It strongly pointed out that information satisfaction plays an important role in mediating the relationship between information characteristics with college choice satisfaction. The result of the study indicated very strongly that information characteristics have no direct impact on college choice satisfaction however; the indirect effect of information characteristics onto college choice satisfaction through information satisfaction is very sizeable (95% confidence interval: 0.534, 0.802). Hence, ultimately the real challenge of marketers of higher education institutions is to ensure that information is disseminated effectively and should result to students being satisfied with such information. As a conclusion, marketers must device their promotional strategies effectively to make sure that potential students are satisfied with the information provided through the various promotional sources.

Keywords: information characteristics, information satisfaction, college choice satisfaction

1   Introduction

Satisfaction level that students have in their college choice can have a long term impact on the continued existence of the college. It has been proven that choice satisfaction is linked to improvement in retention and loyalty rate (Beerli, Martin and Quitana, 2004; Helgesen and Nesset, 2007) and is considered an important performance indicator (Chan and Chan, 2004). Higher education, however, represents a completely new and unfamiliar service experience for students. The advancement in the education services environment has resulted in dramatic changes to the landscape of higher education worldwide and issues pertaining to in-flow and out-flow of students can be very complex. Hence, information on characteristics affecting student satisfaction is essential to marketers. The focus of previous studies on customer satisfaction aimed at understanding satisfaction as a post purchase phenomenon. However, in addition to post purchase satisfaction, it is pertinent to also acknowledge that satisfaction with information may possibly occur before a choice is made. It is reasonable that before a customer can be satisfied with the purchase, one must foremost be satisfied with the information obtained regarding the product/ service. It is during the information search stage that marketers are able to provide the right incitement to influence students regarding their attributes/qualities and create a reaction on needs and wants of potential students leading to positive motivation to a choice decision.

Though, the pursuit of students' search for information on various institutions has been much easier and faster, it has generated a problem of oversupply of information among education institutions. Hence, effective marketing and well-informed communication techniques are considered necessary to influence students not only during their search process but also during evaluation and choice process. With many colleges to choose from, understanding information characteristics influencing these students information satisfaction is significant for administrators of higher education institutions in their marketing management decisions.

Information satisfaction creation could most likely be a major consequence of a purchase behavior. It was indicated that customers perceived different levels of satisfaction with various types of information that was sought and provided by different sources (Li, So, Fong, Lui, Lo and Lau, 2011).This suggests that in addition to comprehending students' information characteristics, effort to find out how satisfied students are with the information acquired should be of crucial concern. In effect, the marketing approaches and students' satisfaction with the information acquired might also have the capacity to influence the choice made, hence choice satisfaction. Information satisfaction provides a better impact and greater insight to the study of students' college choice decision and ultimately their choice satisfaction. This study aims to investigate the relationship between information characteristics, information satisfaction and college choice satisfaction.

2 Literature review

It was argued that students' expectations and satisfaction were to a great extent shaped by the information acquired through various sources (Halstead, Hartman and Schimdt, 1994). And the evaluation between students' expectations and product performance perceptions were based on the information on product attributes/ qualities. Hence, it can be concluded that information gathered from various sources regarding attributes of various colleges was the basis of students' evaluation and judgment. As a matter of fact, it was revealed in a study by Haji Hassan and Mohamad Sheriff (2006) that external marketing stimuli was perceived to be the most dominant determinant in stimulating students' need to pursue their study at higher education institution. The external marketing stimuli mentioned were information regarding college attributes and these attributes among others include quality of programs, quality of lecturers and quality of physical resources. Chapman (1981) also indicated college attributes as important information and were essential criteria for institution choice. According to Wagner and Fard (2009) in their study on Malaysian students' intention to study at a higher education institution, it was found that information on college attributes has a significant relationship with students' intention to pursue higher education.

In addition, due to the massive information provided by various colleges on their attributes, the information accessibility difference among these colleges may also influence the students search process. Accessibility differences may influence how the information is used and thus affect choice outcome. For example, colleges for which information is difficult to acquire or information from web-sites that is difficult to retrieve and comprehend may be ignored and not considered for evaluation of choice. Students may not only prefer information that can be easily obtained but also one that they can comprehend. Hence, in addition to information on college attributes, accessibility issues are of particularly relevant for marketing communication decisions.

Bruce (1998) and Spreng, MacKenzie and Olshavsky (1996) strongly advocated that information satisfaction is an important variable in the judgment of the performance of product used or service employed. They further asserted that the expectation consumers have concerning a product or service is not only depending upon the information gathered. This expectation is also dependent on the feeling of satisfaction with the information they have acquired. Therefore, understanding and identifying information on college attributes that influence students satisfaction with the information acquired will definitely be of great value. This is because by recognizing these attributes marketers will be able to develop better communication and targeting strategies. Especially in education service, which is intangible and is normally associated with high perceived risk (Murray and Schlacter 1990), being satisfied with the information sought enable customers to reduce the level of uncertainty and enhance the quality of choice made.

The satisfaction with information acquired will in turn enhance students' choice satisfaction. Admitting the fact that college choice is the ultimate aim, nonetheless, students' satisfaction with their chosen college is also as important and crucial. Satisfaction is considered an important performance indicator (Chan and Chan, 2004; Selnes, 1993). Customer satisfaction is of importance as it creates new customers and retains current ones. It was proven that customer choice satisfaction was linked to customer retention (Anderson and Sullivan, 1993; Helgesen and Nesset, 2007). And customer loyalty and retention are perceived to be key components of improving market share and enhancing the value of organization (Beerli et al., 2004; Rust and Zahorik, 1993). Peters (in Rust and Zahorik, 1993) pointed out that the cost of new customers may be five times more costly than that of retaining them. Reichheld (1996) indicated that loyalty reduces the need to incur customer acquisition costs. Since it is costly to attract new customers, therefore, retaining existing customers can be very crucial. Satisfied customers will remain loyal and become walking advertisement as through word of mouth (WOM) they talk favorably to others about the service or product.

Hence, in-depth knowledge concerning information characteristics and satisfaction of students is important for education institutions to understand the nature of this process and make better judgment. The above discussion on information characteristics, information satisfaction and choice satisfaction led to the development of the following hypotheses:

H_1 There is a significant relationship between information characteristics and information satisfaction.

H_2 There is a significant relationship between information satisfaction and college choice satisfaction.

H_3 Information satisfaction is a significant mediator in the relationship of information characteristics to college choice satisfaction.

Figure 1 represents the proposed theoretical framework of information characteristics, information satisfaction and college choice satisfaction model. And Table 1 summarizes the conceptual definitions of the variables/ constructs examined in this study.

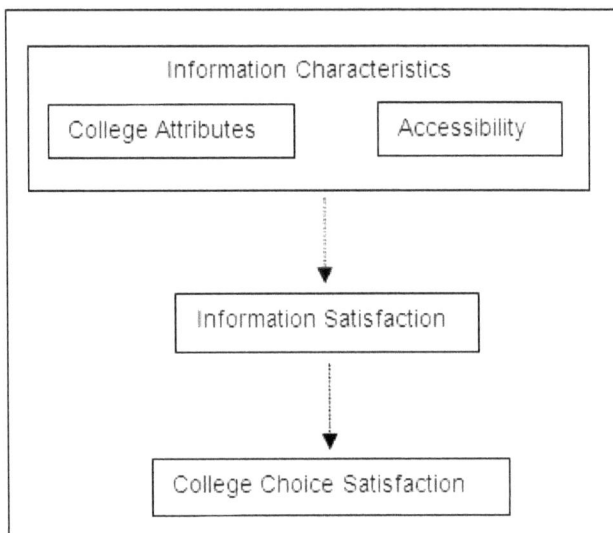

Figure 1: Framework of the study

Table 1: Conceptual definitions

Constructs/variables	Definitions	Sources
Information characteristics College attributes	Characteristics/features of college such as lecturers' quality, location, costs and financial aids, program availability, international recognition and soft skill development. These are antecedents that influence students' satisfaction.	Athiyaman (1997); Bourke (2000); Burns (2006); Chapman (1981); Cubillo, Sanchez and Cervino (2006); Qureshi (1995); Turner (1998)
Accessibility	The extent to which information is available and reachable to the client in a format that the client can use.	Bettman (1979)

Constructs/variables	Definitions	Sources
	Further classified into physical, functional and intellectual accessibility.	Connelly Rich, Curley and Kelly (1990).
Information satisfaction	A subjective satisfaction judgment of the information used in choosing a product.	Spreng et al. (1996)
College Choice Satisfaction	This feeling of contentment will occur when one's expectation are either met or exceeded.	Assael (2001); Oliver (1980)
	Student's positive reaction that comes about when an institution provides an agreeable level of fulfilment in which the institution performance met the student's standard/ expectation.	Ismail (2008)

3   Methodology

This study aims to quantify relationships between variables and to generalize results hence structured questionnaire was employed and self- administered survey approach was used to gather data. Similar approach was used by Helgesen and Nesset (2007) and Letcher and Neves (2010) in their study on student choice satisfaction on higher education institution. The choice of indicators was guided from similar work done by previous researchers as shown in Table 2.

Table 2: List of constructs and sources

	Constructs	No. of items/ indicators	Sources
1	Information Characteristics College Attributes	23	Cubillo et al. (2006); Kusumawati (2010); Wagner and Fard (2009).
	Information Accessibility	9	Connelly et al. (1990)
2	Information Satisfaction	5	Lectcher and Neves (2010); Li et al. (2011); Oliver (1980)
3	College Choice Satisfaction	5	Lectcher and Neves (2010); Mai (2005); Oliver (1980)
	Total	42	

Subjects were international students in various private higher education institutions in Malaysia. Colleges were randomly selected and a proportionate sampling was employed whereby the subjects were divided according to the international students' population and status of the colleges. By employing proportionate sampling, it ensured that the sample size drawn from each group was proportionately represented. This approach was good as it has high statistical efficiency (Cooper and Schindler, 2011 and Saunders, Lewis and Thornhill, 2009).The categorizations of colleges according to their status are university, branch campus, university college and college: The questionnaires were distributed employing three methods based on the type preferred by the officers from the respective colleges. Questionnaires were either hand-delivered, mailed together with a self-addressed stamped envelope or a soft copy of the survey sent via electronic mail. The number of questionnaires distributed to each college was based on the international students' population of the respective colleges. A proportionate number of questionnaires (at least ten percent of the college's international students' population) were given to the officers-in-charge. Finally, out of more than eighty colleges contacted only thirty-two colleges responded and handed over the completed survey within the stipulated time. This whole process took about six months to complete. Out of the 1,915 questionnaires distributed only 620 were collected.

Based on Table 3, the result indicated that sixty-five percent (403 students) of the respondents were male and 35 percent (217 students) of the respondents were female. A majority of the respondents were majoring in the areas of social sciences (57 percent, 356 respondents). The remaining 43 percent (264 respondents) of the respondents were majoring in the area of sciences.

Table 3: Descriptive statistics of respondents' profile

	Frequency	Percentage
Gender:		
Male	403	65%
Female	217	35%
Degree Specification:		
Science	264	43%
Social science	356	57%

Data of 620 samples was checked for major outliers and as a result of data cleaning process, only five cases were identified as outliers and these cases were dropped. The remaining 615 cases were found to be fit for further analysis. Two types of analysis were presented. Firstly, descriptive statistics was employed to describe the basic features of the data for each item in a construct. While the second analyses involved the establishment of the structural model as well as testing the model fit for each construct using structural equation modeling (SEM). Prior to constructing the overall structural model it was necessary to evaluate the goodness of fit measures for each unobserved variables/constructs independently as each construct has multiple-indicators (Anderson and Gerbing, 1988). Table 4 shows the indices that were used to measure the goodness-of-fit for this paper. It also consists of the threshold value for each index. Consequently, modification indexes (MI) were used to alter models to achieve better fit. A few rounds of re-specification were done to improve the validity of each unobserved variable. Though there is no absolute ruling on changing a particular parameter however, the indication is that the decision made on the basis of the MI must be theoretically justified.

Table 4: Indices to measure the goodness-of-fit for this study using SEM

	Goodness of fit indices	Indicator	Source
1	Chi-square and Chi-square/df : as the test for model discrepancy	Less than three (<3)	
2	Goodness of Fit Index (GFI)	More than 0.9 (>0.9)	Byrne (2009); Hair, Anderson, Tatham and Black (2005); Joreskog and Sorbom (1989)
3	Adjusted Goodness of Fit Index (AGFI):	More than 0.9 (>0.9)	Byrne (2009); Hair et al (2005); Joreskog and Sorbom (1989)
4	Comparative Fit Index against the null model (CFI)	More than 0.9 (>0.9)	Bentler (1990); Byrne (2009); Hair et al (2005)
5	Tucker Lewis Index against the null model (TLI)	More than 0.9 (>0.9)	Byrne (2009); Hair et al (2005); Tucker and Lewis (1973)
6	Root Mean Square Error Approximation Index (RMSEA)	Less than 0.08(<0.08)	Browne and Cudeck, (1993); Byrne (2009); Hair et al (2005); Steiger and Lind (1980)

	Goodness of fit indices	Indicator	Source
7	Akaike Information Criterion (AIC): as discrepancy measure between model-implied and observed covariances	The lower the figure the better	Akaike (1973); Byrne (2009); Hair et al (2005); Everitt (2002)

4 Findings, analysis and hypotheses result

4.1 Descriptive statistics

The evaluation of information on college attributes were made in response to the statement "Indicate the importance of the following information on attributes in the choice of a college/university" using a five-point Likert scale anchored by very important to not important at all. Information on college attributes amongst others includes both tangible (hostel, tuition fees, campus environment etc.) and non tangible attributes (reputation, recognition etc.). In general, the mean values for all the 23 indicators were between 3.91 and 4.37 which implied that the information on college attributes were important. Table 5 reveals the three most important indicators.

Table 5: Descriptive statistics for college attributes (top three indicators)

Indicators	Mean	Rank
Good quality education	4.37	1
Reputation of institution	4.31	2
Good campus atmosphere	4.30	3

Measurement for the nine indicators of accessibility was based on the level of agreement on the accessibility of information sought using a five-point Likert scale anchored by strongly agree to strongly disagree. The mean values were at least 3.51 implying that the information was reachable and accessible in a format that students can use. Table 6 reveals the three most important indicators.

Table 6: Descriptive statistics for accessibility (top three indicators)

Indicators	Mean	Rank
The information was available when I needed it	3.75	1
I was able to understand the information well	3.65	2
I was able to simplify the information I've gathered	3.64	3
I was able to analyze the information gathered	3.64	3

Items for both information satisfaction and college choice satisfaction were measured on the degree of student's satisfaction agreement using five-point Likert scales anchored by strongly agree to strongly disagree. All the five indicators of information satisfaction and college choice satisfaction revealed a mean value of at least 3.65 and 3.66 respectively. Hence, it can be concluded that students were satisfied with the information gathered and were pleased with their choice decision.

4.2   Structural model of the study

Figure 2 reveals the structural model for this study. The figure indicates that the model has three main constructs (college choice satisfaction, information satisfaction and information characteristics). Information characteristics were categorized into two sub-domains: attributes and accessibility. And attributes were measured by professional skills and development, issues on education institution, cost and financing and lastly academic programs. Figure 2 also indicates that all the goodness-of-fit statistics met the appropriate acceptable value and the model fit was acceptable. The Chi-square/df was below 3.0, other fix indices were more than 0.90 and RMSEA was less than 0.08.

In addition, based on Figure 2, the factor loading (L) for items in information characteristics construct ranged from 0.67 to 0.83, 0.69 to 0.81 for information satisfaction construct and 0.76 to 0.87 for college choice satisfaction construct. As suggested by Hair, Anderson, Tatham and Black (2005), in the case of multivariate analysis with social sciences, factor loading above 0.50 is required. Hence, when factor loading is more than 0.50, the percentage of variance explained (L^2) will naturally be more than 0.25. Figure 2 reveals the L^2 values of all the items of the constructs for this study exceeded the minimum value. The lowest L^2 value for information characteristics construct is 0.45 indicating that the item was explaining 45 percent of the construct. While the lowest L^2 value for information satisfaction and college choice satisfaction is 0.48 and 0.58 respectively. The result indicated that the overall fit for the model was considered acceptable and appropriate for further analysis.

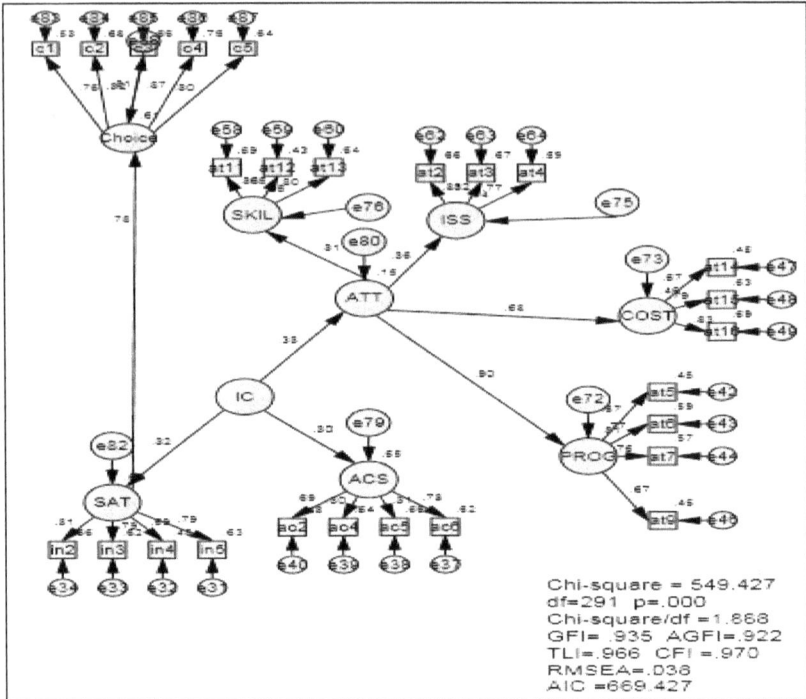

IC = Information characteristics, ATT = Attributes, ACS = Accessibility, SAT = Information satisfaction, Choice = College choice satisfaction

Figure 2: Structural model of the study

4.3   Analysis of hypotheses

As presented in Table 7, findings of this study indicated that the first two hypotheses (H_1 and H_2) were supported and were in congruent with previous literatures. It can be concluded that information characteristics (beta = .851) is an important predictor of information satisfaction and information satisfaction (beta = .781) in turn is an important predictor of college choice satisfaction.

Table 7: Research hypotheses result

		Std.Est	C.R.	P	Beta	Result
H₁	There is a significant relationship between information characteristics and information satisfaction	.448	5.931	**.001***	.851	Supported
H₂	There is a significant relationship between information satisfaction and college choice satisfaction	.045	15.885	**.001***	.781	Supported

*Significant level at 0.05

Figure 3 presents the hypothesized information satisfaction and choice satisfaction model that is assessed. In the structural path of the final model the two endogenous variables are information satisfaction and college choice satisfaction and the exogenous variable is information characteristics. Since information satisfaction is both exogenous and endogenous it is also called the mediator variable.

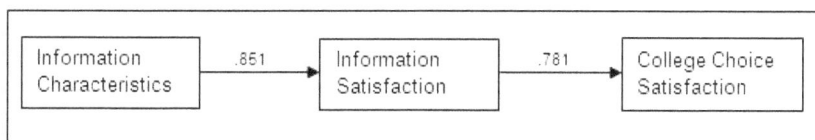

Figure 3: Finalized framework for this study.

H_1 There is a significant relationship between information characteristics and information satisfaction.

The result strongly supported this hypothesis (beta = 0.851, p = 0.001). Both information on college attributes and accessibility of information were of importance in determining the strong agreement of satisfaction with the information. Hence for students, the more important the college attributes were to them the higher their information satisfaction would be if the information gathered met their expectation. As for information accessibility, according to Daugherty and Ellinger (1994), information availability, hence accessibility and clients' responsiveness are positively associated. Brown (2002) and Lederer, Maupin, Sena and Zhuang (2000), further confirmed that the usage of information is highly dependent on the ease of finding and understanding the information itself. With respect to the result, it can be suggested that these international students were not able to physically view the institution hence the ease and accessibility of informa-

93

tion were very important. When information was readily accessible, these students were able to respond and react better and this translated to greater client fulfillment and satisfaction in their information search prior to making a choice.

H_2 There is a significant relationship between information satisfaction and college choice satisfaction.

Result of the study strongly support this hypothesis (beta = .781, p = 0.001) demonstrating that there is a positive direction of relationship between information satisfaction and college choice satisfaction. Result reported is consistent with findings of previous researchers (Bruce, 1998; Halstead et al., 1994 and Spreng et al., 1996). Hence, it can be explicated that students' college choice satisfaction is positively dependent on the information satisfaction. Spreng et al. (1996) examined individual's overall satisfaction with a purchase and found that individual feeling of satisfaction with the choice made is reliant on two antecedents; performance of the products or services and information satisfaction. Hence, this further strengthens the explanation of the relationship between information satisfaction and college choice satisfaction. Evidences from this study pointed out that the more the students are satisfied with the information, the more likely the students will be satisfied with their college choice.

H_3 Information satisfaction is a significant mediator in the relationship of information characteristics to college choice satisfaction.

A further examination was done to test the mediating effect of information satisfaction based on 1,000 bootstrap resamples. Based on Table 8, the value of zero (0) does not fall within the intervals.

Table 8: 95% confidence interval for mediating effect based on 1,000 bootstrap resamples

	Information Characteristics
College choice satisfaction	[0.534, 0.802]

In addition, the regression coefficient for information characteristics and college choice satisfaction is shown in Table 9. The P value of the tested relationship is more than 0.05. Hence, there is no evidence of direct effect of information characteristics on college choice satisfaction. Based on Table 8 and Table 9, results strongly indicated that information satisfaction was a significant mediator in information characteristics to institution choice satisfaction relationship.

Table 9: Regression coefficient for information characteristics and college choice satisfaction

		Std.Est	C.R.	P
Information Characteristics	→ College Choice Satisfaction	.445	1.93	.084

5 Conclusion and discussion

With increasing competition among various education institutions both locally and globally, these institutions need to cautiously re-examine their promotional and communication strategies. Higher education institutions are facing environmental challenges that call for the development of new marketing approaches. Strategically marketers and administrators must acknowledge factors that have significant impact towards students' choice decision. It is of main concern for marketers and administrators of education institutions to provide their potential students with sufficient and relevant information to support their decision. As pointed out by Eagle and Brennan (2007), relying on fundamental marketing concepts, it becomes evident that once institutions identify students' needs and wants, the task of satisfying these needs and wants becomes more feasible. The findings of this study provided two very interesting discovery. Firstly, findings of this study indicated that information characteristics are determinants of information satisfaction and consequently students' choice satisfaction is dependent on information satisfaction. Secondly, result strongly pointed out that information satisfaction plays an important role in mediating the relationship between information characteristics with college choice satisfaction. The result of the study indicated very strongly that information characteristics have no direct impact on college choice satisfaction. However, the indirect effect of information characteristics onto college choice satisfaction through information satisfaction is very sizeable (95% confidence interval: 0.534, 0.802).This significant finding implied that the challenges of marketers are not only to focus on providing information on vital college attributes but as important is also on strategies on how information should be disseminated appropriately and effectively. As postulated by Cardozo (1965), customer expectation about a service or product to a certain degree may be influenced by marketer controlled information disseminating techniques (such as advertisement, catalogues and brochures). Hence, ultimately the real challenge of marketers of higher education institutions is to ensure that information is disseminated successfully and should result to students being satisfied with such information. Result of this study strongly suggested that information satisfaction is a condition for the formation of student's college choice satisfaction.

References

Akaike, H. (1973) "Information Theory and an Extension of the Maximum Likelihood Principle", In B.N Petrov & F. Csaki (Eds). Second International Symposium of Information Theory (pp. 267 – 281). Budapest: Acadamiai Kaido

Anderson, J.C. and Gerbing, D.W. (1988) "Structural Equation Modelling in Practice: A Review and Recommended Two-step Approach", Psychology Bulletin, Vol 103, pp 411 – 423.

Anderson, E.W. and Sullivan, M.W. (1993) "The Antecedents and Consequences of Customer Satisfaction for Firms", Marketing Science, Vol 12, No. 2, pp 125 – 143.

Assael, H. (2001) Consumer Behavior and Marketing Action, 6th edition, Thomas Learning

Athiyaman, A. (1997) "Linking Student Satisfaction and Service Quality Perceptions: The Case of University Education", European Journal of Marketing, Vol 31, No.7, pp 528-540.

Beerli, A., Martin, J. D. and Quitana, A. (2004) "A Model of Customer Loyalty in the Retail Banking Market", European Journal of Marketing, Vol 38, No. 1 / 2, pp 253 – 275

Bentler, P.M. (1990) "Comparative Indexes in Structural Models", Psychological Bulletin, Vol 107, pp 238 -246

Bettman, J.R. (1979) An Information Processing Theory of Consumer Choice, Addison-Wesley Publishing Company Inc.

Bourke, A. (2000) "A Model of the Determinants of International Trade in Higher Education", The Service Industries Journal, Vol 20, No.1, pp 110-138.

Brown I.T.J. (2002) "Individual and Technological Factors Affecting Perceived Ease of Use of Web-Based Learning Technologies in Developing Country", Electronic Journal on Information Systems in Developing Countries, Vol 9, No.5, pp 1 – 15.

Browne, M. W. and Cudeck, R. (1993) "Alternative Ways of Assessing Model Fit", in Bollen, K. A., and Long, J. S. (ed.) Testing Structural Equation Models, Newbury Park, CA: Sage

Bruce, H. (1998) "User Satisfaction with Information Seeking on the Internet", Journal of the American Society for Information Science, Vol 49, No. 6, pp 541-556.

Byrne, B.M (2009) Structural Equation Modeling with AMOS: Basic Concepts, Applications, and Programming, Routledge

Burns, M.J. (2006) "Factors Influencing the College Choice of African-American Students Admitted to the Institution of Agriculture, Food and Natural Resources", Thesis presented to the Faculty of the Graduate School University of Missouri-Columbia.

Cardozo, R.N. (1965) "An Experimental Study of Customer Effort, Expectation, and Satisfaction", Journal of Marketing Research, Vol 11, Aug, pp 244-249.

Chan, A.P.C and Chan, A.P.L. (2004). "Key Performance Indicators for Measuring Construction Success", Benchmarking: An International Journal, Vol 11, No. 2, pp. 203 – 221

Chapman, D.W. (1981) "A Model of Student College Choice", The Journal of Higher Education, Vol 52, No.5, September - October, pp 490-506.

Connelly D.P., Rich E.C., Curley S.P. and Kelly J.T. (1990) "Knowledge Resource Preferences of Family Physicians", Journal of Family Practices, Vol 30, No.3, March, pp 353 – 359

Cox, D.F. (1967) Risk Taking and Information Handling in Consumer Behavior, D.F Cox ed, Boston: Harvard University Press.

Cooper, D.R. and Schindler, P.S. (2011) Business Research Methods, 11th edition, McGraw-Hill International Edition

Cubillo, J.M., Sanchez, J. and Cervino, J. (2006) "International Students' Decision-making Process", International Journal of Educational Management, Vol 20, No. 2, pp 101-115.

Daugherty, P.J. and Ellinger, A.E. (1994) "Information Accessibility: Customer Responsiveness and Enhanced Performance", International Journal of Physical Distribution and Logistics Management, Vol 25, No.1, pp 4- 17.

Eagle, L. and Brennan, R. (2007) "Are Students Customers? TQM and Marketing Perspectives", Quality Assurance in Education, Vol 15, No. 1, pp 44-60.

Evans, M.M, Foxall, G and.Jamal, A. (2009) Consumer Behaviour, 2nd edition, John Wiley & Sons Ltd.

Everitt, B.S. (2002) The Cambridge Dictionary of Statistics, 2nd edition, Cambridge University Press

Hair, J.F., Anderson, R.E., Tatham, R.L., and Black, W.C. (2005) Multivariate data analysis, 6th edition, Englewood Cliffs, NJ: Prentice Hall

Haji Hassan, F. and Mohamad Sheriff, N, (2006) "Students' Need Recognition for Higher Education at Private Colleges in Malaysia: An exploratory Perspective", Sunway Academic Journal, Vol 3, pp 61 – 71

Halstead, D., Hartman, D. and Schimdt, S.L. (1994) "Multisource Effects on the Satisfaction Formation Process", Journal of the Academy of Marketing Science, Vol 22, No.2, pp 114-129.

Helgesen, Ø. and Nesset, E. (2007) "What Accounts for Students' Loyalty? Some Field Study Evidence", International Journal of Educational Management, Vol 21, No. 2, pp 126-143.

Ismail, N. (2008) "International Students' Satisfaction in their Choice of a Private Higher Education Institution", Proceeding of the 9th International Business Research Conference, Melbourne, Australia.

Kusumawati, A (2010) " Privatisation and Marketisation of Indonesian Public University: A Systematic Review of Student Choice Criteria Literature", Proceeding of the Indonesian Student International Conference, Thinking of Home while Away:The Contribution of Indonesian Students Studying Overseas for Education in Indonesia, Melbourne, Australia.

Lederer, A.L., Maupin, D.J., Sena, M.P. and Zhuang, Y. (2000) "The Technology Acceptance Model and the World Wide Web", Decision Support System, Vol 29, pp 269 – 282.

Letcher, D.W and Neves, J.S (2010) "Determinants of Undergraduate Business Student Satisfaction", Research in Higher Education Journal, Retrieved from http://www.aabri.com/manuscripts/09391.pdf

Jöreskog, K.G and Sörbom, D. (1993) LISREL 8: Structural equation modeling with the SIMPLIS command language, Scientific Software International / Erlbaum

Li, P.W.C, So, W.K.W, Fong, D.Y.T, Lui, L.Y.Y, Lo, J.C.K and Lau, S.F. (2011) "The Information Needs of Breast Cancer Patients in Hong Kong and Their Levels of Satisfaction with the Provision of Information". Cancer Nursing, Vol 34, No.1, January/February, pp 49-57.

Mai, L.W (2005) "A Comparative Study Between UK and US: The Student Satisfaction in Higher Education and its Influential Factors", Journal of Marketing Management, Vol 21, pp 859-878.

Murray, K.B. and Schlacter J.L (1990) "The Impact of Services Versus Goods on Consumers' Assessment of Perceived Risk and Variability", Journal of the Academy of Marketing Science, Winter, Vol 18, No.1, pp 51-65.

Oliver, R.L. (1980) "A Cognitive Model of the Antecedents and Consequences of Satisfaction Decisions", Journal of Marketing Research, Vol 17, November, pp 460-469.

Peters, T. (1988) Thriving on Chaos, New York, NY, Alfred A Knopf.

Qureshi, S. (1995) "College Accession Research: New Variables in an Old Equation", Journal of Professional Services Marketing, Vol 12, No. 2, pp 163-170.

Reichheld, F.F. (1996) The Loyalty Effect: The Hidden Force Behind Growth, Profits, and Lasting Value, Harvard Business School Press, Boston, MA.

Rust, R.T. and Zahorik, A.J. (1993) "Customer Satisfaction, Customer Retention, and Market Share", Journal of Retailing, Vol 69, No. 2, pp 193-215.

Saunders, M., Lewis, P. and Thornhill, A. (2009) Research Methods for Business Students, 5th edition, Financial Times Prentice Hall.

Selnes, F. (1993) "An Examination of the Effect of Product Performance on Brand Reputation, Satisfaction and Loyalty", European Journal of Marketing, Vol 27, No. 9, pp 19 – 35

Spreng, R.A., Mackenzie, S.B. and Olshavsky, R.W. (1996) "A Reexamination of the Determinants of Consumer Satisfaction", Journal of Marketing, Vol 60, July, pp 15-32.

Steiger, J.H. and Lind, J.C. (1980) "Statistically Based Tests for the Number of Common Factors", Paper presented at the Psychometric Society Annual Meeting, Iowa City, IA, USA.

Tucker, L.R and Lewis, C. (1973) "A Reliability Coefficient for Maximum Likelihood Factor Analysis", Psychometrika, Vol 38, pp 1-10

Turner, J.P. (1998) "An Investigation of Business Undergraduates' Choice to Study at Edith Cowan University", Unpublished research report, Edith Cowan University, Perth

Wagner, K and Fard, P.Y. (2009) "Factors Influencing Malaysian Students' Intention to Study at a Higher Education Institution", Paper presented in: E-Leader Conference Kuala Lumpur, 5-7 January, Retrieved from http://www.g-casa.com/PDF/malaysia/Wagner-Fard.pdf

Online Formative Assessment: Does it add up to Better Performance in Quantitative Modules?

Elena Fitkov-Norris and Becky Lees
Kingston University, London, UK
Originally published in ECRM (2012) Conference Proceedings

Editorial Commentary
This study tackles the question of whether university students perform better when participating in summative assessment or formative assessment methods taking end of the year exams. The specific scope of this paper addressed university students majoring in Business Administration. Numerous statistical methods, including but not limited to retrospective multivariate regression, collinearity testing and ridge regression. Although the findings of this study are in line with previous studies, including that by Angus and Watson in 2009, the current study adds to the body of knowledge with its inclusion of standardized regression coefficients and collinearity diagnostics.

Abstract: Students who follow a social science programme often find quantitative methods challenging. Poor numeracy skills impact upon performance of tertiary education students, particularly in the first year of their programme, and since first year performance has the greatest impact upon retention (Yorke 2005), supporting students to develop their numeracy skills early on in higher education is vital. Previous studies concentrating on the use of online formative assessment methods to support learning in quantitative modules report positive benefits, and that exposure to online formative tests is sufficient to enhance subsequent summative exam performance (Angus and Watson 2009). Given these benefits a similar assessment framework was implemented on a first year quantitative methods module taken by approximately 400 business students, many of whom have not taken any mathematical studies since their GCSEs. The aim of this study was to consider whether student participation in a series of online formative assessments had an impact upon overall performance on this module, both within the formative tests and subsequent summative exam. This empirical study analysed the participation and performance data from a cohort of business students, taking into consideration their level of prior attainment, extrinsic motivation, gender and age. A retrospective ridge regression model was fitted and used to examine the nature of the relationship between participation and performance in online formative assessments and overall module attainment, as preliminary analysis identified high collinearity between formative test participation and formative test grades. The results suggest that this data set does not support the hypothesis that participation, rather than performance, in formative assessment is a better predictor of student end-of-year exam performance. However, there is evidence that although small, the impact of participation in formative assessment on end of year assessment is positive and significant. Furthermore, the study confirmed that prior attainment in quantitative modules is a significant predictor of future attainment, particularly for male students and that student motivation plays a significant part in overall achievement.

Keywords: online formative assessment, performance, evaluation, quantitative methods

1   Introduction

Assessment forms an indelible and sometimes controversial part of education, with claims of over-assessment in schools making appearances in headlines with predictable regularity. Although not subjected to the same scrutiny, the subject of assessment in higher education has also attracted considerable attention. The changing nature of higher education in terms of raised expectations, larger classes and more diverse student populations has lead to more research into the efficacy of existing assessment and the introduction of more innovative assessment methods (Bartram and Bailey 2010). This in turn has lead to the foregrounding of the different types of assessment, with the majority of all discussions focused on the relationships between summative and formative methods of assessment.

Summative assessment is widely agreed to be a form of evaluation that provides a judgment which encapsulates all the evidence up to a given point, usually the end of a teaching period (Taras 2005). It is a powerful tool that has the purpose of providing a student with a grade, thus enabling them to be differentiated amongst their peers (Wininger 2005). The research on summative assessment methods exposes several criticisms of the approach. (Yorke 2005) leads a discussion as to whether students' final achievements are adequately represented by summative assessment methods, in particular as to the scale of the final awards. The other major criticism of summative assessment is that it focuses too much on 'How did I do?' rather than 'How am I doing?' (Kibble et al. 2011), which supports the now extensive body of research into methods of formative assessment that help students develop as learners (Yorke 2005) and permit interventions during learning rather than after learning has taken place (Black and Wiliam 1998).

If an assessment method provides a student with an opportunity to gauge their progress whilst there is time to rectify any lack of understanding, it starts to take on a formative role rather than a summative one. Since the seminal review on formative assessment methods by (Black and Wiliam 1998), the definition of formative assessment has been discussed, debated and developed through several iterations, all of which have the intention to improving student learning at their core.

Several studies suggest that formative assessment must provide fast feedback in order to be useful, although this might cause tensions given the fact that there has been a shift towards modularisation and semesterisation in UK HE, causing reduced timeframes for the provision of feedback (Yorke 2005; Bartram and Bailey 2010). The implications of time and implementation requirements in a shorter timeframe has helped encourage the development of online assessment methods a 'low-cost, reusable, customisable and scalable initiative' (Armellini and Aiyegbayo 2009) and although this approach carries a fixed overhead, it is better suited for a mass approach to higher education than more traditional methods (Yorke 2005) and in general students are receptive to the use of online assessment methods (Dermo 2009).

Many quantitative studies confirm that formative assessment contributes positively to gains to student understanding and achievement (Black and Wiliam 1998; Angus and Watson 2009; Dobson 2008; Kibble et al. 2011) and employability (Yorke 2005). However, some research studies report less favourably on the benefits of formative assessment and there are examples of contradictory results of the effect of formative assessment on performance (Dunn and Mulvenon 2009). Therefore, the research would suggest that formative assessment could be both constructive and inhibitory for learning achievement (Yorke 2005). Part of the reason for the lack of clarity over the effects of formative assessment may relate to confusion in the extent to which an assessment event is classed as either formative or summative (Bennett, 2009; Yorke, 2005; Taras, 2008) and difficulty in its definition and understanding given the term formative has been open to misinterpretation (Bennett, 2009) and often seen as an add-on to regular teaching and learning methods rather than an integral part of the overall strategy (Yorke 2005).

The purpose of this paper is to examine the impact of frequent formative assessment on student performance and examine the validity of this as a support tool for the learning of students on a general business degree participating in a quantitative methods module. It is recognised that students who follow a social science based programme find quantitative methods challenging (Murtonen and Lehtinen 2003) and this awareness has encouraged research into the effectiveness of frequent formative assessment in supporting student's learning. Of particular interest is a large-scale study by Angus and Watson (2009), which concluded that it is exposure to, rather than performance in, frequent online formative assessment, which has a significant positive impact on end-of-module examination scores for students on a business mathematics module. This empirical study will test if data from a large sample confirm Angus and Watson's (2009) findings by analysing the participation and performance data from a cohort of business students, controlling for level of prior attainment, motivation and gender biases. This study aims to further Angus and Watson's (2009) work by attempting to assess the relative predictive power of performance and participation in frequent online formative tests in end of year exam performance.

2 Educational context

The Quantitative Methods module is offered as a core module for all year one students across a range of programmes ranging from general business management to specialist programmes such as: Marketing, Human Resource Management or Accounting and Finance. The assessment for this module consists of unseen end of module exam and individual coursework. The exam comprises of two sections: a multiple choice questions section which covers the entire module content and an in-depth questions section which allows students to demonstrate more detailed knowledge on topics covered in the module. The coursework is a case study which assesses students' critical analysis skills. The overall module mark also includes a small contribution from four formative assessment tests which the students complete online. Each test can be taken twice so a student unhappy with their first grade has an opportunity to improve it. Test questions are drawn at random from a large question bank so a student taking the test for the second time will not be answering questions identical to their first attempt.

The sample consists of 462 students who sat the end of year exam and summarises the number of formative tests they attempted, their average grade from the tests and exam grade, together with their gender, type of degree (general business, specialist or Accounting and Finance), length of degree (3-year or 4-year depending on their intention to do a placement) and age at the start of the module. The additional indicator variables for gender, type of degree (general business, specialist or Accounting and Finance), length of degree (3-year or 4-year) were added to align the analysis more closely with a similar study done by (Angus and Watson 2009).

The average grade attained by student in the end of year exam is 60%, the formative test grade is 65% and the majority of students attempted all 4 formative tests (Table 1).

Table 1: Number of formative tests attempted

Number of Formative Tests Attempted				
		Frequency	Percent	Valid Percent	Cumulative Percent
Valid	0	10	2.2	2.2	2.2
	1	16	3.5	3.5	5.6
	2	31	6.7	6.7	12.3
	3	109	23.6	23.6	35.9
	4	296	64.1	64.1	100.0
	Total	462	100.0	100.0	

A slightly larger proportion of male students (51.5%) sat the exam. The majority of students (53.5%) have registered for a general business degree (i.e. Business Management, Business Administration, Business Studies), 33.5% have enrolled on specialist degrees (Marketing, Human Resource Management) and 13% of students in the sample have enrolled on an Accounting and Finance (A&F) degree. Accounting and Finance students are required to have achieved at least a grade B at GCSE Mathematics, while all other students have achieved the lower requirement of at least a grade C at GCSE Mathematics. The degree type would be used as a control variable for prior attainment in Mathematics. Its effect may be somewhat mitigated as there could be students who enrolled on a general or specialist business degree who may have attained at better GCSE Mathematics grade, however, gathering information about students exact entry qualifications poses practical and ethical challenges.

The indicator variable for degree length (3-years or 4-years) depending on whether the student intends to do a work placement or not, is included as a control for the extrinsic goal orientation of the students (Midgley et al. 1998). Students who enrol on the 4-year version of the degree would be motivated to impress potential employers with their year one grades, while students on the 3-year version have no such incentive as the year graded do not count towards final degree classification under current regulations. The majority of students in the sample (69%) enrolled on the 3-year version of their degree.

The mean, median, and mode age of the students is 19, with 79% under the age of 21.

3   Research design

Retrospective multivariate regression methodology was used to investigate the potential predictive impact of number of formative tests attempted and the test grades on end of year exam performance. Exam grade (%) was entered as the dependent variable, while participation in number of formative tests and average formative test grade (%) were input as independent variables, together with additional indicator variables for gender, degree type (general, specialist or A&F) and degree length (3-year or 4-year). As mentioned earlier degree type is used a proxy for prior attainment in Mathematics, while degree length is a proxy for students extrinsic motivation. The analysis was carried out using PASW Statistics 18.0 and estimated the coefficients for the following equation.

Final Exam Grade = β_0 + β_1x Formative Test Grade + β_2x Number of Formative Tests Attempted
+ β_3 x Degree Type + β_4 x Degree Length + β_5 x Gender

This paper sets out to test if the sample data supports the following hypothesis:

The number of formative tests attempted, rather than the grade attained in these is a good predictor of students' performance in the end of year exam.

Initial investigation of the data showed that the number of tests attempted and the average formative test grade are highly correlated, and a collinearity test was performed as part of the regression analysis. This identified high multicollinearity between number of formative tests attempted and formative test grade as the Variance Inflation Factors (VIF) for both number of tests and test grade were greater than 2 (both in the region of 3.4) and their respective condition indices are greater than 15 which are the suggested as benchmark values for the presence of multicollinearity in PASW statistics. Collinearity is a problem that leads to the estimation of unstable regression coefficients, which should not be interpreted. Removing either number of tests or the test grade from the model is not an option, as the objective is to compare the impact of the two variables on exam grade. Therefore, the coefficient estimates for the regression function were estimated using a ridge regression approach.

Ridge regression has been identified as a suitable approach for dealing with multicollinearity and identifying both stable regression coefficients and significant variables (Marquardt and Snee 1975). Ridge regression introduced a penalty term to the standard regression equation with a coefficient lambda, which acts as bias in the estimates, and often significantly reducing the variance of the estimated model coefficients. The regression equation is then run for different values of lambda and an optimal value for lambda is chosen by using standard cross validation or bootstrapping techniques (Marquardt and Snee,1975; Hoerl and Kennard, 1970).

PASW Statistics provides the ridge regression technique in combination with optimal scaling and categorical regression. This approach has the added advantage of identifying optimal scales for the nominal and ordinal variables in the model. The ridge regression analysis was run with a .623 bootstrap estimate that collected 50 samples. The optimal value for lambda was 0.56. The results were validated by running the analysis at several random starting points all producing very similar solutions.

Table 2 shows the optimal scaling (transformed values) of the independent variables as identified by PASW Statistics.

Table 2: Transformed values for independent variables

Variable	Scale	Discretization	Transformed values
Exam grade	Numeric	N/A	Numeric
Number of Test	Ordinal	N/A	0 tests = − 4.57 1 test = − 3.42 2 tests = −.81 3 tests = .09 4 tests = .39
Formative Test Grade	Ordinal	Intervals length 10	10 equal intervals
Degree Type (general, specialist or A&F)	Nominal	N/A	General = −.31 Specialist = −.51 A&F = 2.58
Degree Length (3- year or 4- year)	Ordinal	N/A	3-year = −.67 4-year = 1.49
Gender	Nominal	N/A	Male = −.97 Female = 1.03

Table 3 shows that the transformation of formative test grade and number of tests attempted increased the tolerance of the two independent variables, and collinearity diagnostic tests confirm that collinearity is no longer a problem. Therefore, the estimated coefficients can now be interpreted. Zero order correlations confirm the correlation between the transformed independent variables and the transformed exam grade with formative test grade is moderate to strong ($r = .582$), while the correlation between transformed exam grade and transformed number of tests attempted is moderate ($r = .366$). The partial correlations confirm that formative test grade is the most significant predictor of variance in exam grade (20%), if the effect of all other variables is eliminated from both the end of year exam grade and the formative tests grade. All remaining predictors explain a small amount of variance in exam grade once the effects of all other independent variables are removed - around 2% each for degree type and degree length, and less than 1% each for gender and, surprisingly, number of tests attempted. This suggests that the formative test grade is the most significant predictor of end of year exam performance as the proportion of variation in exam performance explained by the number of tests attempted is also explained by the other independent variables included in the model.

Table 3: Correlations and tolerances

	Correlations and Tolerance				
	Correlations			Tolerance	
	Zero-Order	Partial	Part	After Trans-formation	Before Trans-formation
Degree type (general, special-ist, A&F)	.221	.175	.141	.930	.950
Degree length (3-year or 4-year)	.112	.114	.091	.988	.991
Formative test grade	.582	.454	.404	.588	.311
Number of tests attempted	.366	.034	.027	.606	.315
Gender	.088	.097	.078	.982	.973
Dependent Variable: Exam grade					

The results from the ridge regression analysis presented in Table 4 show that overall the independent variables explain 36% of the variance in exam grade, with all independent variables being statistically significant.

Table 4: Ridge regression coefficients (penalty .56, .632 bootstrap estimate with 50 samples).

	Coefficients				
	Standardized Coefficients				
	Beta	Bootstrap (1000) Estimate of Std. Error	df	F	Sig.
Degree type (general, specialist, A&F)	.112	.022	2	25.900	.000
Degree length (3-year or 4-year)	.062	.023	1	7.628	.006
Formative test grade	.307	.018	8	299.015	.000
Number of tests attempted	.108	.020	4	28.523	.000
Gender	.049	.023	1	4.455	.035
Dependent Variable: Exam grade					

Although none of the coefficients are particularly large, formative test grade is the most significant predictor of exam performance, with one standard deviation increase in formative test grade yielding a .307 increase in the standard deviation of exam grade. Number of tests attempted and degree type are second in terms of their impact on exam performance with one standard deviation increase in number of tests and degree type leading to around .11 increase in the standard deviation of exam performance. As a nominal variable, the coding of degree type needs to be interpreted alongside the optimal coding recommended by PASW.

As it can be seen from Table 2, increasing the level of prior achievement in mathematics of students, from GCSE Grade C for general business and specialist degrees to Grade B for Accounting and Finance students, leads to an increase in the expected exam performance. The impact of degree length and gender on exam performance is rather small. The data suggests that increasing the degree length from 3 years to 4 years leads to an almost negligible increase in the standard deviation of exam grade. The effect of gender (moving from male to female) is similar to the effect of degree length in both direction and magnitude.

The interaction effects between the independent factors, namely degree length (3-year or 4-year), gender and degree type (general, specialist or Accounting & Finance) and the dependent variable (end of year exam performance) were also examined. The only significant interaction occurred between gender and degree length. While the mean exam grade for females did not depend on whether they had chosen a 3 or a 4-year degree, the mean exam grade for males who chose the 4-year version of their respective degree was significantly better than the mean grade for males who chose the 3-year version. This suggests that degree length controls for the intrinsic motivation in male students better that than in female students.

There also seems to be some weak interaction between gender and degree type. Although not statistically significant, the mean final exam performance of male students on the Accounting & Finance degree was better than females, while on the specialist and general business degrees, females outperformed their male counterparts. This suggests prior attainment in mathematics is perhaps more significant in predicting future success in male students. Further, qualitative research, may shed further light on these interaction effects and their relationship to overall performance.

4 Results and discussion

The results show that the most significant predictor of end of year exam performance for this sample of students is formative test grade, followed by number of formative tests attempted and the students' prior achievement in mathematics which have small, but significant impact. Gender and degree length (3-year or 4-year degree) all have negligible effect on exam performance, although they are all statistically significant. Overall the, variables explain approximately 36% of the variation in end of year exam performance.

These finding are in line with previous findings that frequent participation on formative assessment has a positive impact on student summative achievement (Yorke 2005; Wininger 2005; Angus and Watson 2009). However, the data do not support the hypothesis derived from Angus and Watson's (2009) study that it is participation in, rather than performance in frequent formative assessment that is the most significant predictor of student performance. The formative test grade achieved has a larger influence (.316) on end of year exam performance than number of tests attempted (.109). Although direct comparison with Angus and Watson's (2009) findings is difficult since they did not report their standardised regression coefficients, it is clear that the magnitude of the test participation coefficient estimate is much larger. This could be partly due to the fact that the current study attempts to evaluate the incremental impact of test participation, with test participation rates ranging from 0 to 4, while Angus and Watson (2009) presented test participation as an indicator variable (0, if student attempted up to and including 3 tests, and 1 if the student attempted all 4 tests). In addition, their study does not seem to have encountered the problem of collinearity as they did not report any collinearity diagnostics. Although they considered marks achieved by students in previous mathematics courses rather than the actual online test grade in their study it would have been helpful to see those. Although not presented here, a collinearity diagnostics test was run for the collinearity between formative test grade and number of formative tests attempted, coded as an indicator variable at the same scale as Angus and Watson (2009) and these indicated that collinearity is still present.

As expected, the impact of previous mathematics attainment on end of year exam grade is positive and this finding is inline with the conclusions reached by Angus and Watson (2009). This is further confirmed by carrying out an Independent Samples Kruskal-Wallis test which showed that there is no significant difference in the mean number of formative tests attempted across the different degree types (general, specialist or A&F). Despite this, Accounting and Finance students attained significantly better results in both formative test grades and the end of year exam grade, than both the specialist and general business students. There was no significant difference in the formative test or end of year exam performance of students enrolled on a general business or a specialist business degrees. Furthermore, interaction between degree type and gender suggests that prior attainment in mathematics is more significant in predicting future success on a quantitative module for male students, rather than females.

The main impact of gender on end of year exam performance is very small, with female students performing slightly better than male students. Gender is not a significant differentiator of performance in the formative tests, however the evidence suggest that girls tend to participate in significantly higher number of tests than boys when an Independent Samples Mann-Whitney U Test is carried out. This seems to lend support to the positive impact of participation in formative assessment on performance, as other research has suggested that females tend to under perform in quantitative subjects (Hargreaves et al. 2008).

The additional variable included in this study - degree length, which reflected whether a student is expecting to do a placement or not, has a very small impact on end of year exam performance, with students on the 4-year version of the programme performing slightly better than students on the 3-year version. This difference in performance is statistically significant as confirmed by an Independent Samples Mann-Whitney U Test. The variable was included as an indicator to students' extrinsic motivation and the results suggest students who choose the 4- year version may be motivated to do better. This is particularly evident for male students who seem to perform significantly better than the male students on a 3- year version of their respective degrees. This could be because they are aware that good year one results could contribute to getting a placement. On the other hand, it is possible that students who choose the 4-year version of a programme have greater motivation from the onset to make the most from their university experience. This point warrants some further investigation.

5 Conclusions

This paper set out to establish whether the data sample from a year one quantitative methods module in a UK business school supports the hypothesis that it is the number of formative tests attempted rather than the formative test grade that is a better predictor of end of year exam performance. Ridge regression analysis, taking into account additional indicator variables such as gender, prior attainment and degree length was used to estimate the impact of number of tests attempted and formative test grade on exam performance. The results suggest that this data set does not support the hypothesis that it is participation, rather than performance in formative assessment that is a better predictor of student performance in end of year exams. However, there is evidence that, although small, the impact of participation in formative assessment on summative end of year assessment is significant and positive and therefore, there is some merit in using online formative tests as part of a quantitative methods module. The study confirmed that prior attainment in a quantitative module is also a significant predictor of future attainment, with weak evidence that this relationship is more pronounced for male students. In addition, the analysis suggested that motivation plays a significant part in overall achievement and this is particularly relevant for male students. The factor interaction effects suggest that practitioners need to be keenly aware of the different motivational levels of male students who do not have prior achievement in mathematics and may lack strong intrinsic motivation as they are at the greatest risk of underachieving on a quantitative module.

The results demonstrate the complex nature of the relationships between formative online test participation and end of year exam performance and highlight the need for further more in-depth research in this area.

Acknowledgements

The authors would like to thank Dr David Martland for his helpful suggestions and advice.

References

Angus, S.D. and Watson, J. (2009) "Does regular online testing enhance student learning in the numerical sciences? Robust evidence from a large data set", British Journal of Educational Technology, 40, No. 2, pp 255–272.

Armellini, A. and Aiyegbayo, O. (2009) "Learning design and assessment with e-tivities", British Journal of Educational Technology, 41, No. 6, pp 922–935.

Bartram, B. and Bailey, C. (2010) "Assessment preferences: a comparison of UK/international students at an English university", Research in Post-Compulsory Education, 15, No. 2, pp 177–187.

Black, P. and Wiliam, D. (1998) "Assessment and classroom learning", Assessment in Education: Principles, Policy & Practice, 5, No. 1, pp 7–74.

Dermo, J. (2009) "e-Assessment and the student learning experience: A survey of student perceptions of e-assessment", British Journal of Educational Technology, 40, No. 2, pp 203–214.

Dobson, J.L. (2008) "The use of formative online quizzes to enhance class preparation and scores on summative exams", AJP: Advances in Physiology Education, 32, No. 4, pp 297–302.

Dunn, K.E. and Mulvenon, S.W. (2009) "A critical review of research on formative assessment: The limited scientific evidence of the impact of formative assessment in education", Practical Assessment, Research & Evaluation, 14, No. 7, pp 1–11.

Hargreaves, M., Homer, M. and Swinnerton, B. (2008) "A comparison of performance and attitudes in mathematics amongst the "gifted." Are boys better at mathematics or do they just think they are?", Assessment in Education: Principles, Policy & Practice, 15 No. 1, pp 19–38.

Hoerl, A. E., and Kennard, R. W. (1970) "Ridge regression: applications to nonorthogonal problems", Technometrics, 12, No. 1, pp 69–82.

Kibble, J.D. et al. (2011) "Insights Gained from the Analysis of Performance and Participation in Online Formative Assessment", Teaching and Learning in Medicine, 23, No. 2, pp 125–129.

Marquardt, D.W. and Snee, R.D. (1975) "Ridge regression in practice", American Statistician, 29, No. 1, pp 3–20.

Midgley, C. et al. (1998) "The development and validation of scales assessing students' achievement goal orientations", Contemporary Educational Psychology, 23, pp 113–131.

Murtonen, M. and Lehtinen, E. (2003) "Difficulties experienced by education and sociology students in quantitative methods courses", Studies in Higher Education, 28, No. 2, pp 171–185.

Taras, M. (2005) "Assessment—summative and formative—some theoretical reflections", British Journal of Educational Studies, 53, No. 4, pp 466–478.

Wininger, S.R. (2005) "Using your tests to teach: Formative summative assessment", Teaching of Psychology, 32, No. 3, pp 164–166.

Yorke, M. (2005) "Formative assessment in higher education: Its significance for employability, and steps towards its enhancement", Tertiary Education and Management, 11, No. 3, pp 219–238.

Polarization in Research Methods Application: Examining the Examiner

Edwin Asiamah Acheampong, Marcia Mkansi, Kondal Reddy Kondadi and Baomin Qi
University of Bolton, UK
Originally published in ECRM (2012) Conference Proceedings

Editorial Commentary
This paper investigates the age-old controversy of research philosophies and approaches. In particular, does the preferential approach by university supervisors/examiners possibly interfere with the students' development of sound research, and if such turmoil exists, should the university step in immediately to resolve the conflict? Whilst the authors pose very interesting questions and performed due diligence in obtaining a goodly number of subjects for their study, the response rate was in fact abysmal. Rather than ignore this fact, the authors face it head-on by explaining that the controversial subject may well have played a role in the lack of participation in the study by university faculty subjects. The authors also comment on the apathetic nature of most supervisors/examiners on the research methodology discourse. Although this analogy may be correct, the interesting topic hypothesized by the authors, and the information gleaned in the study well warrant further investigation into this interesting and important topic.

Abstract: This paper emerges as a reaction to the assertion of polarization or dichotomies in research method. The aim is to find out whether this assertion by some writers of research methods application, 'hold water' within academia. To that extent, the study designed a survey questionnaire to elicit the opinions of PhD supervisors and examiners from three North West region of England: University of Bolton, Salford, and Manchester. The study addresses the issue of polarization in research methods by investigating whether some researchers become dogmatic in the application of research method through supervision and examination of prospective researchers, PhD students? If so, what does that posture represents? Can a supervisor-student relationship be marred by these preferences? This research paper attempts to answer these questions from supervisors'/examiners' perspective. A purposive and referral sampling methods were adopted to reach supervisors, who otherwise, would have declined to partake in such an incisive study. The findings of the study confirm some of the relationships between research philosophies and research approaches, and most importantly reveal the sentiments of the surveyed population on the apparent rivalry between research philosophies and approaches. Furthermore, the paper presents the candid observations and opinions of the writers on the qualitative/quantitative debate. The major limitation of the study is the abysmal response from the surveyed universities. This will in no doubt detract from the overall impact of the findings of the study.

Keywords: examiner(s), supervisor(s), polarization, qualitative research, quantitative research, research philosophy

1 Introduction
Research methods, essentially, are to give the researcher the needed mechanism to carry out effective investigation in his/her field of study. A research method largely defines the design of the problem under investigation (Saunders et al., 2009; Khotari, 2006; Kumar, 2011). Whatever the preferred research method, there are three distinct main approaches to addressing any research problem: Qualitative, Quantitative, and mixed methods (Bryman, 2006). This means that based on the approach, a research study can be either qualitative, quantitative or a mixture in nature. These research approaches and their application have their roots in one research philosophy or the other. In other words, the research philosophy which defines the assumptions constructed about the phenomena of interest and so predefines the ontological, epistemological and methodological scope of the study (Guba and Lincoln, 1994; Ritchie and Lewis, 2003). Thus, according to Bryman (1984), much of the research literature considers, to some extent, the research philosophy to determine, by and large, which approach the researcher should adopt. It is therefore fairly straight forward to determine the likely approach of a study from the underlying philosophy.

On the basis of research philosophies, researchers identify themselves as interpretivist, positivist, critical realist, pragmatist, etc.; with their differences, at the lowest ebb, separating or grouping them into those who espouse the qualitative methods (Caelli et al., 2003 ; Seale, 1999); those who predominantly approach research problems quantitatively (Sharf, 1995; Polit and Beck, 2008); and those who consider a blend of the two approaches as the best option (Johnson and Onwuegbuzie, 2004; Howe, 1988) .

Speaking on the dichotomy between quantitative and qualitative methods in his book, *Doing Qualitative Research*, Silverman (2010), notes, "In the context of this book, I view any such dichotomies or polarities in social sciences as highly dangerous. At best, they are pedagogic devices for students to obtain first grasp on a difficult field; they help us to learn the jargons. At worst, they are excuses for not thinking, which assemble groups of researchers into "armed camps", unwilling to learn from one another'. The scholar continues, 'the fact that simple quantitative measures are a feature in some good qualitative research shows that the whole "quantitative/qualitative" dichotomy is open to question'.

Saunders et al. (2009), point out that there is nothing like pure quantitative study or pure qualitative study. Again, Sekaran and Bougie (2010), explain that the choice of a quantitative or qualitative method should be informed by the type of investigation under consideration. Debates have been ongoing, tackling which method is better than the other. The reason why this remains unresolved until now is that each has its own strengths and weaknesses which actually vary depending upon the topic the researcher wants to discuss. (Experiment-resources.com, 2009)

Miles and Huberman (1994) agree that quantitative and qualitative research methods need each other more often than not. In their book *Qualitative Data Analysis*, quantitative researcher Fred Kerlinger is quoted as saying "There's no such thing as qualitative data. Everything is either 1 or 0". As if responding directly to Fred Kerlinger's assertion, researcher D. T. Campbell, states "all research ultimately has a qualitative grounding". Miles and Huberman (1994), note that the quantitative/qualitative debate is to all intents and purposes fruitless.

There are fundamental differences between quantitative and qualitative methods. Typically, qualitative data involves words and quantitative data involves numbers. Qualitative research is inductive and quantitative research is deductive (Saunders et al., 2009). Again, in qualitative research, a hypothesis is not needed to begin research. However, all quantitative research requires a hypothesis before research can begin. Does this make one more scientific than the other?

This study surveys the opinions of PhD supervisors and examiners in the Greater Manchester locality of North West England on the subject and their views on the impact such an inclination could have on supervisor-student relationships. More specifically, the study will answer the following questions:

Q1. Do supervisors/examiners' philosophical inclinations make them prefer one research approach to the other?

Q2. How do supervisors/examiners view the qualitative/quantitative debate?

Q3. How do supervisors/examiners feel about an inclination towards a particular research method?

It is expected that the findings of this incisive study will add to the debate while presenting the opinion of an important constituency on the issue.

2   Methodology

2.1   Sampling
Three universities, Bolton, Salford and Manchester, were targeted for the study but only supervisors and examiners from the universities of Bolton and Salford participated. The sampling frame was the databases of all PhD supervisors and examiners within the three universities. With the exception of a few survey questionnaires that were administered face-to-face, the bulk of the questionnaires were mailed to the supervisors and examiners via their university email addresses. In all, over ninety questionnaires were administered to the three universities. No response came from the University of Manchester and the remaining two universities produced only ten responses. The response rate was thus slightly above 11%. A good comprehension of survey practice which guided this study can be found in (Kelly et al., 2003; Krosnick, 1999; Sanders et al., 2009).

2.2 Participants

All the ten respondents were PhD Supervisors, with three doubling as examiners as well. Two of the supervisor-cum-examiners were professors from the social sciences and engineering faculties and the third, a doctor, also from the social science faculty. Thus, many more supervisors participated in the study than examiners. Majority of respondents have worked as supervisors between one and five years. Six of the respondents were from Bolton and four from Salford.

2.3 Data collection

A carefully worded survey questionnaire was designed to elicit the views of supervisors and examiners for the study. There were a couple of demographic variables. Respondents were asked to indicate their title, gender, number of years as a supervisor/examiner and their faculty.

The questions were generally centred on research philosophy and its implication for PhD students' research projects. Most of the questions were closed-ended. Written answers were to be provided for the few open-ended questions. The questionnaire took about ten minutes to complete but this was no incentive to attract satisfactory participation.

2.4 Procedure

Confidentiality of responses and anonymity of respondents were clearly communicated and so respondents completed the questionnaires based on informed consent. Respondents returned the completed via emails soon after completion. Three questionnaires were administered in person. No incentive was given for participation.

2.5 Results

All responses were coded and analyzed with SPSS. Being as study to survey perception and opinion, only simple frequencies and cross tabulations were run on the data collected.

2.6 Frequencies

As noted earlier the response rate was abysmal, with only ten supervisors and examiners choosing to participate against an expectation of between fifty and seventy respondents. So the results provided represent the views of a minority in the studied universities. This downside notwithstanding, the results are worth communicating given the incisive character of the study.

The ten respondents came from the social sciences and engineering faculties. Other faculties targeted were the Humanities, Health Sciences and the Sciences. Three respondents identified themselves as primarily interpretivist, positivist or critical realist. The remaining seven saw themselves as espousing a combination of the research philosophies. All respondents claimed that their choice of research philosophy (ies) is based wholly on personal reasons. Probing this claim to know when personal reasons inform a supervisor's research philosophy would have been interesting as a parallel study showed that almost all PhD students' acclaimed philosophical stance is informed by their research approach. Only a few attribute their philosophical stance to their supervisors' leadings.

Twenty percent of respondents indicated that they were qualitative researchers. Ten percent, on the other hand, were inclined to both approaches with each treated as an independent approach based on the research problem at hand. The rest of the respondents did not have any inclination towards either of the approaches. Their views corroborate advocates of either of the approaches, whether seale's (1999) qualitative, or Polit and Beck's (2008) quantitative. They would go along with a blend of the two, as echoed by Johnson and Onwuegbuzie's (2004). Eighty percent of respondents agree that an inclination towards a particular research philosophy could lead to polarization of research methods, where a supervisor/examiner may have strong preference for a particular method to the neglect of others. In the same vein, majority of respondents believe that a supervisor-student relationship may be affected negatively if there is an inclination towards a particular research method. Such a tendency, if negatively pursued, could limit the student's research experience and is likely to breed discontent and disagreements.

With respect to students' research projects, the respondents indicated that supervisors and examiners attraction to particular research methods could lead to negative consequences if not managed well. These may include:

- Wrong outcomes
- Wastage of resources
- De-motivation of students

Respondents were unanimous in their call for institutional intervention if supervisors' and examiners' inclination towards particular research methods leads to strong disagreements.

Respondents indicated categorically that supervisors and examiners should not at any point impose their research method preferences on their students. This reflects the awareness of half of respondents who have witnessed supervisor-student relationships that have turned sour because of disagreements on the choice of research methods. The weird incidence of a supervisor/examiner insisting on a particular research method(s) without regard to the subject under investigation or the student's research objectives has been witnessed by only 10% of respondents.

The assertion by Silverman (2009) that a researchers' inclination to particular research methods is an excuse for refusing to learn from one another was put to the test. Eighty percent of the respondents agreed with the assertion. The remaining two did not respond to the question. Proffering their opinion on how supervisors and examiners can be convinced to be more tolerant of other research methods they may not find appealing, the responses included open mindedness of supervisors and examiners, personal learning and supervisors and examiners becoming active reviewers of academic journals. This comes alongside the opinion of others who believe convincing supervisors and examiners who might have such stance would be a difficult task.

The qualitative/quantitative debate is indeed not likely to end in any time in the foreseeable future. Fifty percent of respondents believe there are pure qualitative or quantitative methods that do not consider the other in any conceivable way. This opinion comes in sharp contrast to that of the other fifty percent of respondents who are of the opinion that there is not such study as pure qualitative or pure quantitative.

A summary of the comments made by respondents with regard to study includes:
- Open and continuous discussion on the subject is necessary
- The war between philosophies and paradigms in unnecessary
- The qualitative/quantitative debate is overplayed
- A timely study

2.7   Cross tabulations

With cross tabulations various views are combined to obtain insights that may not be apparent from the raw frequencies. For instance, all respondents who identified themselves as interpretivists were from the social science faculty. This finding unconsciously captures the 'novel gospel' preached by Interpretivist advocates including Babbie (2007). Whereas the respondent that claims to be positivist is from the engineering faculty. This relation endorses the assertion of some researchers that positivists are inclined to the sciences (Alvesson and Skoldberg, 2009). Four respondents from the social sciences and one from the engineering faculties indicated that they espoused more than one research philosophy. It was also insightful that the two respondents who opined that they are inclined towards qualitative research approach were from the social sciences faculty as this has been the claim widely (Babbie, 2007). There was no direct relationship between the research philosophies and the research approaches. All respondent who identified themselves as interpretivists had no special preference for the qualitative approach. In fact, as note earlier, majority of respondents had no inclination towards the qualitative or quantitative approach or a blend of the two.

It is notable that the two professors who participated in the survey did not identify themselves with any particular research philosophy though they belonged to different faculties.

3   Discussions

By and large, the literature on research methods associates the interpretivist philosophy with the qualitative approach (Babbie, 2007; Seale, 1999). In the same vein, the social sciences including IT-based programmed are said to be largely interpretive and hence inclined towards the qualitative approach. Given the major setback of the study, however, this trend is perceptible from the findings of the study. Table 1 gives a cross-tabulation outlook of the respondents' faculty and adopted research philosophy.

The scientists are generally considered positivists (Alvesson and Skoldberg, 2009), and there may be a confirmation of this fact by the respondent from engineering faculty who identified himself as such.

Table 1: Respondents' faculty and espoused philosophy

		Research Philosophy				
		Interpretivist	Positivist	Critical Real-ist	Other	Total
Faculty	Social Scienc-es	3	0	0	4	7
	Engineering	0	1	1	1	3
	Total	3	1	1	5	10

Another critical observation is the split-decision on whether there are re-search methods that are 'pure' qualitative or quantitative in nature. The fifty percent of respondents who did not believe anything like 'pure' quali-tative or quantitative studies included all the respondents who identified themselves as interpretivist, positivist or critical realist. Only respondents who espouse a blend of philosophies have come across such 'pure studies'. None of the literature surveyed for this study underscored such strict ap-plication of approaches in a research study. It would therefore be insightful if further studies will delve into this research methods and studies that are wholly or strictly qualitative or quantitative in nature.

From the findings, there is no gainsaying that a supervisor's/examiner's inclination towards a particular research method could have a positive or negative consequence on a student's research work. According to views expressed in the study, institutional intervention should be swift if strong disagreements ensue as a result of such inclinations. But how many stu-dents would like to incur the displeasure of their supervisors or examiners by resisting their 'determined intrusion', as far as, their research methods are concerned? This remains a research question.

The abysmal response rate cannot be glossed over. The writers of this pa-per would want to believe the subject area is a slippery turf for some su-pervisors and examiners. In fact, some supervisors who did not respond to the survey questionnaire were of the opinion that the questions were 'strong'. Others misconstrued the intentions of the writers to mean 'an attack' on supervisors and examiners. However one interprets this hitch in the study, most of the non-respondents cannot be absolved from a 'calcu-lated attempt to frustrate the study'. It is against this backdrop that the writers agree with suggestions from respondents to have an open and con-tinuous discussion on the subject matter.

4   Conclusion

This short study has presented the opinions of supervisors and examiners on a sensitive debate. A revelation from the three universities studied is that most supervisors and examiners are apathetic to such a discourse. Perhaps, organisers of conferences such as the European Conference of Research Methods should facilitate discussions on research methods in universities so that supervisors and examiners can engage with students on such a 'potentially distractive' subject matter.

This study, in no doubt, will contribute its quota to the quantitative/qualitative debate, which stem from the established philosophies and paradigms. The association between the interpretivist and positivist philosophies and qualitative/quantitative dichotomy was observable. Again, the relationship between science and non-science faculties and their inclined research philosophies was revealed by the study.

While some of the respondents referred to the qualitative/quantitative debated (and by extension, their underlying philosophies) unnecessary and unfruitful, the fact still remains that students would have to justify their research methods at one time of their studies or the other. Thus, continuous engagement on the issue cannot be trivialised.

As trumpeted throughout the study, the major limitation of the study is the abysmal response rate; only ten out of over ninety survey questionnaires administered received feedback from supervisors and examiners in the studied universities. A more representative response would have projected the true position of supervisors and examiners on the subject under investigation. The writers were unable to adopt any corrective measures due to the brevity of time. Nonetheless, the apparent sensitive nature of the study makes the findings from the study worth disseminating and discussing.

It is recommended that in future studies, measures should be taken to secure the best of responses from supervisors and examiners so that finding would be largely representative of the universities studied.

References

Alvesson, M. and Skoldberg, K (2009) Reflexive Methodology: New Vistas for Qualitative Research. Sage.

Babbie, E. (2007) The practice of social research.Thomson Wadsworth.

Bryman, A. (2006) 'Integrating quantitative and qualitative research: how it is done?'. Qualitative Research, Vol. 6, No. 1, pp. 97-113.

Bryman, A. (1984) 'The debate about Quantitative and Qualitative Research: A question of Method or Epistemology? The British Journal of Sociology, Vol. 35, No. 1, pp.75-92.

Caelli, K.; Ray, L.; Mill, J. (2003) 'Clear as Mud: Toward Greater Clarity in Generic Qualitative Research'. International Journal of Qualitative Methods, Vol. 2, No, 2.

Guba, E. G. and Lincoln, Y. S. (1994) Competing Paradigms in Qualitative Research, Handbook of qualitative research. Sage.

Howe, K. R. (1988) 'Against the Quantitative-Qualitative Incompatibility Thesis or Dogmas Die Hard'. Educational Researcher, Vol. 17, No.8, November, pp. 10-16.

Johnson, B. R. and Onwuegbuzie, A. J. (2004) 'A Research Paradigm Whose Time Has Come'. Educational Research, Vol. 33, No. 7, pp. 14-26.

Kelly, K.; Clark, B.; Brown, V.; Sitzia, J. (2003) 'Good practice in the conduct and reporting of survey research'. International Journal for Quality in Health Care, Vol. 15, No. 3, pp. 261-266. Oxford University Press.

Khotari, C. R. (2006) Research Methodology: methods and techniques. New Age International (P) Ltd., 2nd Ed.

Krosnick, Jon, A. (1999) 'Survey Research'. Annual Reviews Psychology, Vol. 50, pp. 537-67. Annual Reviews.

Kumar, R. (2011) Research Methodology: A step-by-step Guide for Beginners 3rd Ed. Sage Publications, Ltd.

Martyn Shuttleworth (2008). What is Research?. Retrieved 26 Jan. 2012 from Experiment Resources: http://www.experiment-resources.com/what-is-research.html [11 January 2012]

Miles and Haberman (1994) Qualitative Data Analysis: An Expanded Sourcebook 2nd Ed. Thousand Oaks, Sage.

Polit, D. and Beck, C., T. (2008) Nursing Research: Generating and Assessing Evidence for Nursing Practice. Lippincott Williams and Wilkins.

Ritchie, J. and Lewis, J. (2003) Qualitative research practice: a guide for social science students and researchers. Sage.

Saunders, M.; Lewis, P.; Thornhill, A. (2009) Research Methods for Business Students. Pearson Education Limited, 5th Ed.

Scharff, R. C. (1995) Comte After Positivism. Cambridge University Press.

Seale, C. (1999) 'Quality in Qualitative Research'. Qualitative Inquiry, Vo. 5, No. 4, pp. 465-478 (1999). Sage

Sekaran, U. and Bougie, R. (2010) Research Methods for Business: A skill building approach. Wiley.

Silverman, D. (2010) Doing qualitative research, 3rd edition. Sage, London.

The Pervasiveness and Implications of Statistical Misconceptions Among Academics with a Special Interest in Business Research Methods

Frank Bezzina[1] and Mark Saunders[2]
[1]Department of Management, Faculty of Economics, Management and Accountancy, University of Malta, Msida
[2]Surrey Business School, Faculty of Business, Economics and Law, University of Surrey, Guildford, UK
Originally published in EJBRM (2013)

Editorial Commentary

This paper states that although the topic of student conceptions and misconceptions relating to research methodologies is well researched, there is a lack of research addressing this topic in regard to academics. The basis for this study is to investigate whether misconceptions relating to the nature of research is prevalent among academics and to what extent these individuals hold differing conceptions of research practice. The findings for this study were quite interesting and although it is apparent from the findings that differing conceptions are prevalent amongst the academics questioned, some worrisome issues emerged relating to ethical issues in research. The authors further discuss the problematic environment that may eschew from such misconceptions of research methods by academics.

Abstract: Statistics play a very important role in business research, particularly in studies that choose to use quantitative or mixed methods. Alongside statistical analysis, aspects related to research design (such as sampling, reliability and validity issues) require a good grounding in statistical concepts reinforced by careful practice to avoid potential mistakes arising from statistical misconceptions. Although quite a considerable number of published studies have focused on students' faulty thinking regarding statistical concepts, little research explores the extent to which these are also held by academics who are their instructors. This empirical study addresses this by answering the following questions: First, are statistical misconceptions pervasive among academics with a special interest in business research methods? If so, second, is there an association between the pervasiveness of statistical misconceptions and the preferred research tradition (qualitative, quantitative, mixed methods)?. Data were collected via a web questionnaire from a purposive sample of academics with an expressed interest in business research methods. The questionnaire comprised 30 categorical statements (agree, disagree, don't know) focusing on statistical misconceptions (and conceptions) relating to descriptive statistics, design strategies, inferential statistics and regression, and five demographic questions. We targeted a critical case purposive sample of 679 potential respondents. Although 166 consented to take part, only 80 completed the questionnaire and their responses form the basis of the statistical analysis, a response rate of 11.8 %. The study provides empirical evidence of both an absence of knowledge and a high pervasiveness of faulty notions that have infected the thinking of academics relating to both research design and the use of statistics. This is particularly so for academics who prefer quantitative methods, those preferring qualitative methods being more likely to admit that they do not know. The study argues that such lack of knowledge and misconceptions reduce the true utility of statistics in research. Recommendations are offered regarding the teaching of statistics within business research methods.

Keywords: research methods, misconceptions, conceptions, statistics, academics, research practice

1   Introduction

Statistical misconceptions are argued to hinder meaningful learning, impede research progress and interfere with decision making (Huck, 2009). For students, such misconceptions may be generated by poor understanding reinforced by statements uttered or written by one's mentors (Huck, 2009). The study seeks to determine whether academics with a special interest in business research methods hold mainstream statistical misconceptions, thereby extending a recent study that investigated the prevalence of research methods mis/conceptions with the same target group (Bezzina & Saunders, 2013). To date, limited research has examined the pervasiveness of statistical misconceptions among academics; the studies we reviewed focused on either identifying students' statistical misconceptions (e.g., Bezzina, 2004; Huck, Cross & Clark, 1986; Mevareck, 1983) or statistical flaws made by authors in published articles, reports and textbooks (e.g. Huck, 2009; Lance, 2011; von Hippel, 2005). Consequently, this research enables academics to determine whether faulty thinking has infected academics' notions about mainstream statistical concepts and considers the impact of these on their students. In addition, in the light of the findings that emerge, this paper provides some important suggestions for the teaching of business research methods, particularly on what the state of practice should be.

2   The nature of misconceptions and the role of academics

Misconceptions are "views or opinions that are incorrect due to faulty thinking or misunderstanding" (Bezzina & Saunders, 2013, p. 41)", representing deviations from widely accepted norms and conventions. In some cases, the practices themselves are not intrinsically faulty but rather, it is the reasoning why or rationalisation used to justify the practices that is questionable (Lance & Vandenberg, 2009).

Misconceptions arise from prior learning or from interacting with the social/physical world and interfere with learning concepts (Smith, diSessa & Roschelle, 1993). Some are grounded in human intuition that leads to faulty thinking, while others are generated by inconsistencies in textbooks and oral presentations in classrooms (Huck, 2009). Garfield (1995, p.32) highlights that misconceptions are often so strong and resilient that "they are slow to change even when students are confronted with evidence that their beliefs are incorrect". Similarly, Mevareck (1983) argues that when statistical misconceptions become deeply engrained in the underlying knowledge base of the individual, mere exposure to more advanced courses is not sufficient to overcome them. However, Brown and Clement (1989) note that successful instructional confrontation can replace faulty misconceptions with new expert knowledge in a short period of time while Smith, diSessa and Roschelle (1993) advise that the emphasis should be on knowledge refinement and reorganisation rather than replacement. Given that faulty thinking is such a pervasive phenomenon, it is important that academics as instructors are aware of their own misconceptions and the impact of these upon their students (Bezzina & Saunders, 2013).

3 Statistical data analysis and statistical misconceptions

Statistical data analysis is the process by which data are transformed with the aim of extracting useful information and facilitating conclusions. Each statistical technique has underlying conceptual and statistical assumptions that must be met if the results are to be valid (Gel, Miao & Gastwirth, 2005). Various structured-model building approaches and step-by-step guides are available to facilitate this process of data analysis. The scope behind them is to provide researchers with "a broader base of model development, estimation and interpretation" (Hair et al., 1998. p. 25) not a rigid set of procedures to follow. Structured approaches do not come without criticism. Conflicting viewpoints arise on various aspects such as the required sample size, the statistical model to analyse the data, and the quality of the input data.

The statistical mis/conceptions addressed in this study are grouped under following headings: descriptive statistics, design strategies, inferential statistics and regression. Sentences presented in italics represent actual statements used in the research.

3.1 Descriptive Statistics

"A crucial human skill is to be selective about the data we choose to analyse and, where possible, to summarise the information as briefly and usefully as possible" (Graham, 1994, p.64). *A concise way of summarising a data set is to use an appropriate measure of central tendency* (a value that indicates where the centre of the distribution lies) *accompanied by a measure of spread* (a statistic that determines how clustered or scattered the data are). The type of measure chosen ultimately depends on the scale of measurement being used and the shape of underlying distribution (Graham, 1994). A common reported misconception in textbooks and published research reports is that *if a set of scores forms a positively skewed distribution, the mean is greater than the median, which is greater than the mode; and similarly, if a distribution of scores is negatively skewed, the mean is less than the median which is less than the mode.* This rule is imperfect and most commonly fails in discrete distributions where the areas to the left and right of the median are not equal (von Hippel, 2005). Applying this misconception could allow researchers to make wrong judgements on the distributional shape by assessing lack of symmetry of a distribution via measures of central tendency rather than by means of a numerical index of skewness (Huck, 2009). Another misconception related to the shape of the distribution is that *standard scores such as z-scores are normally distributed*. This incorrect generalisation occurs where researchers are unaware that no finite distribution is exactly normal (Huck, Cross & Clark, 1986), and can result in inaccuracies when z-scores are converted to percentiles (Huck, 2009).

In summarising bivariate relationships, the correlation coefficient is generally used (e.g., Pearson's *r,* Spearman's *ρ*, and correlation ratio (eta). However, checks need to be made to see if the data are appropriate (e.g. whether or not the relationship is linear and whether outliers are present). A widely reported misconception is that *a single outlier will not greatly influence the value of Pearson's r, especially when N is large*. However, a single outlier can distort the nature and strength of *r* even when *N* is large. Consequently, Huck (2009) highlights the importance of conducting a visual or statistical check to see if any outliers are present. Another misconception is that *correlation never implies causation*. Huck (2009, p. 48) provides evidence that when a correlational study involves a manipulated variable and there are no plausible threats to internal validity, then "the correlation coefficient, *r*, speaks to the issue of cause and effect". He adds (2009, p.45) that data can be analysed in different ways and still give the same results; thus the warning 'correlation ≠ cause' "functions to keep the logical and mathematical equivalence of certain statistical procedures hidden from view".

4   Design Strategies

4.1   Sampling

An important step in planning of a statistical investigation is sample selection. This requires careful thinking (Lenth, 2000). A small sample is likely to produce a statistic of inadequate precision and makes the statistical test insensitive due to 'low' statistical power. Although an increase in sample size leads to an increase in precision, a very large sample makes the statistical test overtly sensitive (i.e. the identification of an effect relatively easy) due to 'too much' statistical power. Thus, the researcher must strike a balance between the level of statistical error and resulting power (Hair et al., 1998).

Sampling methods are generally classified into probability methods (utilizing some form of random selection) and non-probability methods (Saunders, Lewis & Thornhill, 2012). In this study, we focus on the random aspect of probability sampling, where each element of the population has a known, but possibly non-equal chance of being included in the sample. Within probability sampling, the *sample size determines precision, the selection process determines accuracy*. The following are the questionnaire items related to sampling:

1. *A random sample is a miniature replica of the population.* Statistical representativeness is generally achieved through random sampling (Thomas, 2004). However, a representative sample does yield a miniature repica (or exact replica) of the population. This is because the characteristics of a random sample are not error-free estimates of the population necessitating the specification of confidence intervals (Huck, 2009; Krzywinski & Altman, 2013). *Every sample* (even if generated in a random fashion) *possesses sampling error, provided the population is not totally homogeneous or the sample size is equal to the population size*. Huck (2009) argues that persons holding this misconception make various inferential mistakes.

2. Similarly, *a sample of individuals drawn from a finite population deserves to be called a random sample so long as (i) everyone in the population has an equal chance of receiving an invitation to participate in the study and (ii) random replacements are found for any of the initial invitees who decline to be involved.* This statement is also a misconception because those who choose not to participate are often different from those who participate. The probability of a person responding depends on factors such as age, level of education, interest in the topic being studied and free-time available. If replacements are made, those who are not willing or able to participate are replaced by willing and able respondents. Hence, only a subsection of the population is actually represented and "any sample-to-population inferences will be distorted" (Huck, 2009, p. 129).

3. The statement *larger populations call for larger samples sizes and hence the ratio of sample size to population needs to be considered when determining sample size* is also a misconception. By definition, the precision of a sample depends on the sampling error and the larger sample, the smaller the sampling error, the

greater the precision. However, the standard error formula shows that when *N* is much larger than *n*, the ratio of *n* to *N* does not influence the standard error to great extent. The precision of sample size is more influenced by *n*. Those who hold this misconception would wrongly dismiss the findings of a study if they believe that the sample was too small when compared to the size of the population (Huck, 2009).

4. Finally, the statement *a large sample does not guarantee validity* is correct. The common misconception is that the size of the sample guarantees validity. However, there is more strength (lack of bias) in fewer but well-chosen numbers (van Belle, 2008).

4.2   Reliability and Validity

Errors play a key role in degrading the quality of measurements. Two key issues related to the quality of measurements are reliability and validity (Murphy & Davidshofer, 2004). Reliability refers to the extent to which measures are repeatable and consistent. Validity is the degree to which measures accurately represent what they are supposed to conceptually measure. This study addresses the following mis/conceptions related to reliability and validity:

1. The statement *statistical indices of reliability and validity document important attributes of an instrument (e.g. test or questionnaire)* is incorrect. These indices of reliability and validity document important properties about the scores obtained from the instrument for a particular sample. If a person thinks that these are attributes of the test, then "a researcher may end up selecting what seems to be a good test for his or her study when in fact the selected test produces low-quality data" (Huck, 2009, p. 68).

2. The statement *a high value of Cronbach's alpha indicates that a measuring instrument's items are highly interrelated, thus justifying the claim that the instrument is uni-dimensional in what it measures*, is also flawed. Cronbach's alpha is a measure of internal consistency. Consequently, a high value of Cronbach's alpha does not indicate that the variables used are uni-dimensional (Hair et al., 1998). Even multidimensional instruments often yield high values of Cronbach's alpha. The resultant problem from this misconception is that the total score will not be interpreted correctly. As Huck (2009, p. 78) notes "high or low scores may be

attributed to one thing when they are actually the result of something else". Rather, other specific techniques such as multitrait-multimethod matrix (MTMM), factor analysis (EFA or CFA), structural equation modelling (SEM) and related statistical procedures (see Westen & Rosenthal, 2003) need to be used to determine the dimensionality.

3. *Different procedures for estimating inter-rater reliability yield approximately the same reliability coefficients and so it does not make much difference which procedure is used* is flawed because various factors can affect inter-rater reliability. These include (i) whether or not chance agreement is considered, (ii) whether or not a dichotomy is imposed on the continuum, and (iii) whether or not the raters are considered a random sample from a larger population. The implication of this misconception is that a person using a particular procedure might think that raters are in close agreement with each other when in fact this is not the case when a different and more appropriate perspective is used (Huck, 2009).

4. A common misconception is that *if Pearson's r is used to determine the predictive validity, range restriction will cause r to underestimate the strength of the relationship between the predictor and criterion variables.* However, it is possible to 'correct' for range restriction when the data are linear and homoscedastic. Data collected in real validity studies are not usually very symmetric, and correlations that are corrected for restriction are more likely to exaggerate rather than underestimate r_N. Consequently, persons holding this misconception are likely to use a formula to "correct" for range restriction which inflates Pearson's *r*, thus making them think that predictive validity is higher than what the original coefficient suggested (Huck, 2009).

4.3 Handling missing data

Although there are misconceptions concerning the need for high response rates, Newman (2009) provides evidence that low response rates (e.g., below 20%) need not invalidate study results but systematic (non-random) non-response will generally lead to bias in parameter estimates. Since almost any research has the potential for missing data, van Belle (2008) highlights that *in a research study it is important to plan for missing data and to develop strategies to account for them* prior to the initiation of the study.

Furthermore, when the reasons for missing data are not identified, it is not possible to make statistical adjustments. However, s*ensitivity analyses are* purposely *designed to explore a reasonable range of explanations in order to test the robustness of the results*. Various creative statistical approaches have been developed to deal with missing data (see Cole, 2008).

4.4   Testing of statistical assumptions

Statistical methods rely on a variety of assumptions about the nature of underlying data. When the assumptions are not met, the results are often not valid (Gel, Miao & Gastwirth., 2005). This is crucial as those who are not aware of the related assumptions for a particular test may erroneously assume results are significant. A *violation of the statistical assumptions affects the significance level of a test* as well as the power of the test (Box & Tiao, 1964).

5   Inferential statistics

Inferential procedures are used to derive conclusions about a population. Both estimation and hypothesis testing are concerned with a parameter θ (theta) and may be considered as two sides of a coin. In estimation, *a statistic is an estimator of the true population parameter* θ if its intention is to be close to the unknown value of θ. Optimal estimators are derived according to criteria such as unbiasedness, equivariance and minimaxity (see Lehmann & Casella, 1998, for more details). *A confidence interval* is constructed to *give[s] an estimated range of values around the statistic that are believed to contain with a certain probability (e.g., 95%) the unknown population parameter* (Field, 2009). Hypothesis testing is a procedure that involves (i) setting up a null and alternative hypotheses, (ii) defining the test procedure including the levels of significance and power, (iii) calculating the test statistics and the p-value and (iv) making a decision on whether to retain or reject the null hypothesis. In the process, researchers are required to consider two types of statistical error. *The Type I error (α)*[alpha] *refers to the probability that one mistakenly rejects a true null hypothesis (i.e. a "false positive")*. The Type II error (β) [beta] refers to the probability that one mistakenly retains a false null hypothesis. The statistical power of a test is the probability of not making a Type II error and represents the odds that you will observe a treatment effect when it occurs. As power is increased, the chance of finding an effect if it's there increases; but this also increases the chance of making a Type 1 error. Since researchers aim for high power (e.g., 0.80) and low alpha (e.g., 0.05), and these do not add up to 1, there is an in-built tension here (Trochim, 2000). As alpha decreases, power decreases as well. So in determining power, the researcher must consider three factors simultaneously – alpha, sample size and effect size (Hair et al., 1998). The p-value is the probability of obtaining sample data that deviates as much or even more than the actual data observed, provided the null hypothesis is true (Huck, 2009). When the p-value is less than or equal to the probability of a Type I error, the null hypothesis is rejected and a statistically significant finding is reported. A statistically significant finding is not necessarily practically significant. *Practical significance* or effect size is the magnitude of the effect of interest in the population and *is focused on the study's possible impact on the work of practitioners or other researchers* (Hair et al., 1998). Thus, while it is incorrect to attach adjectives blindly (e.g., strong or weak) on the basis of p< 0.05, Cortina and Landis (2009) argue that it is even incorrect to attach adjectives blindly on the basis of Cohen's *d*. They (2009, p. 306) add that one is likely to choose the appropriate language for effect sizes when "one takes into account sample size...considers the measures involved, the nature of manipulation and the nature of the phenomenon in question".

The following is the list of misconceptions related to inferential statistics used in our study:

1. *The p-value is the probability that the null hypothesis H_0 is true* is clearly a misconception. The p-value is a random variable that varies from sample to sample and it is not the same as alpha (Good & Hardin, 2009). It is a conditional probability and hence should not be confused with alpha (Hubbard, 2004). According to Huck (2009), such faulty thinking produces errors when a null hypothesis is evaluated and in making everyday decisions based on probabilities.

2. The statement *when the whole population is used, no inferential statistics are required since the statistical summary of the data represents a parameter rather than a statistic* is flawed because inferential statistics do not require the population to have finite size. According to Fisher (1922), the goal of inferential statistics is to construct "a hypothetical infinite population" and the actual data collected is regarded as constituting a random sample (see Hacking (1979) and Seidenfeld (1979) for some interesting discussions). Thus, the true population of interest extends from the present into the future or into geographical areas not repre-

sented in the study and so persons holding this misconception wrongly assume that when data is collected from all N members of a population, a statistical summary of the data (e.g., a measure of central tendency or a percentage) produces a parameter not a statistic (Huck, 2009).

3. Similarly the statement *statistically significant results signify strong relationships between variables or big differences between comparison groups* is wrong. Effect size is concerned with the actual magnitude of the effect of interest and not statistical significance. Results which are statistically significant might not be practically meaningful while results which are not statistically significant might have a noteworthy effect size. Ellis (2010) warns that failure to distinguish between statistical and practical significance leads to Type 1 and Type 2 errors, wasted resources and potentially misleads future research on the topic.

4. Likewise, the statement *a non-directional alternative hypothesis always leads to a two-tailed test whereas a directional alternative hypothesis always brings about a one-tailed test* is faulty. With certain statistical tests, the nature of the alternative hypothesis depends on the sampling distribution of the test statistic. For instance, in the Chi-squared (χ^2) test and the ANOVA *F*-test, non-directional alternative hypotheses do not lead to two tails (split critical regions), as in the case of the *t*-test. Huck (2009) argued that persons holding this misconception will not be able to interpret properly the data-based p-value associated with the particular test used.

5.1   Regression

Regression is one of the most widely used statistical techniques and this is not limited to business and management research. It is used to predict the likelihood or magnitude of the outcome of interest and to explore relationships and assess contributions. Various types of regression models exist (e.g., linear regression, non-linear regression, multiple regression, logistic regression, etc.). In this study, we address the following four misconceptions concerning multiple regression analysis.

1. The statement *when multiple regression is used to predict scores on a criterion variable, the worth of a particular variable is indicated by the variable's beta weight (i.e., its standardized beta co-*

efficient) is faulty. *In multiple regression, any statistical relationship between two variables may be altered by additional variables* (Meyers, Gamst & Guarino, 2005). When a new predictor is introduced in the model, variables can take a new level of importance within the expanded model, depending on the predictors included in the model and the degree of overlap between variables (Tolmie, Muijs & McAteer, 2011). The implication of this is that an estimated beta coefficient is not the true value of a given predictor variable. As Huck (2009) explained, double the dose of chilli powder in a recipe and the impact of the other ingredients such as onions and beans (which previously played a prominant role) is significantly reduced. Hence it is important that when researchers interpret the beta weight, they do so relative to the specific model that produced it.

2. Likewise the statement *in multiple regression, an independent variable that is uncorrelated with the dependent variable ought to be left out of the model because its inclusion won't help to make the coefficient of determination (R^2) larger* is incorrect. Sometimes some variables which are uncorrelated with the dependent variable help to reduce the error variance in the other predictors; their inclusion better explains the variability in the criterion variable. Researchers holding this misconception are likely to eliminate such "suppressor" variables and hence they would end up with a model that falls short of its potential (Huck, 2009).

3. Finally the statement *regression analysis is superior to correlational analysis* is misconceived. This statement runs counter to the assertion that there is no univerally superior research design (Bryman, 2012) and that the research question is more important than either the method or the paradigm that underlines the method (Shavelson & Towne, 2004; Teddlie & Tashakkori, 2010). All statistical techniques have their strengths and weakness; some are simple while others are complex, but often very specific for certain purposes. Each statistical technique is a tool not an aim and hence the statistical technique chosen ultimately depends on (or is dictatated by) the research question being investigated, not vice-versa.

5.2   Research Paradigms

In the social sciences, research is very often divided into the qualitative camp and the quantitative camp. There has been an on-going debate on the distinction between the two. There are those who claimed that the distinction between the two is by no means clear (Bryman & Bell, 2011; Lincoln & Guba, 1985) while others argued that quantitative and qualitative traditions are so different in their epistemological and ontological assumptions as to be incompatible (Hammersley, 1992; Robson, 2011). According to Eby Hurst and Butts. (2009), the proponents of qualitative research make strong claims that their approach has greater ecological validity, that it provides richer and more descriptive accounts of real-world events and has a greater ability to uncover processes and mechanisms in natural settings, while the proponents of quantitative research emphasise their approach is advantageous due to strengths in the precision of measurement, experimental control and generalizability. Alongside the qualitative versus quantitative debate, there has been growing recognition of mixed-methods, which combine the qualitative and quantitative traditions (Bryman, 2006). In mixed methods, both deductive and inductive techniques may be selected and integrated to answer the research question or solve the problem be it theory testing or theory generation (Teddlie & Tashakkori, 2010).

6   Method

6.1   Research Questions

This study considers the following two research questions empirically:

1. Are statistical misconceptions pervasive among academics with a special interest in business research methods?
2. If so, is there an association between the pervasiveness of statistical misconceptions and the preferred research method (qualitative, quantitative, mixed methods)?

6.2   Procedure

The target population consisted of academics who are members of the Research Methodology Special Interest Groups (RM SIGs) of either the British Academy of Management (BAM) or the European Academy of Management (EURAM) (540 people), or have attended the European Conference on Research Methodology (ECRM) at least once in the past three years (139), an estimated total of 679 potential respondents after accounting for multiple list membership. A questionnaire was created using the Survey Monkey online tool. The front page provided respondents with information regarding the research, requested their consent, and assured them of anonymity. The main questionnaire consisted of 30 randomly ordered categorical statements representing statistical mis/conceptions. Respondents were requested to tick one from 'agree', 'disagree' or 'don't know', the latter being included to avoid forcing the respondents to provide a response when they did not have such knowledge. The statements are presented in Table 1, the majority being adapted from Huck (2009) while the remainder were adapted from Box and Tiao (1964), Field (2009), Good and Hardin (2009), Hair et al. (2008), van Belle (2008) and von Hippel (2005). The final section requested demographic information about the respondents. Respondents were able to amend their responses until the questionnaire was submitted, while the software restricted one respondent per work station to prevent multiple completions. The e-mail with weblink targeted 679 potential respondents. 166 questionnaires were returned (24.4%), but 86 respondents although consenting to take part, reported that they 'don't do quants' or the questionnaire was too 'complex', 'confusing' or 'tricky'. This resulted in 80 complete returns (a response rate of 11.8%) that formed the basis of the statistical analysis. The questionnaire took approximately 10 minutes to complete. The preferred research method of the respondents was qualitative (47.5%), followed by mixed methods (27.5%) and quantitative (25.0%). The single largest groups were male (51.2%), those in possession of a doctoral degree (70.0%), those based in the United Kingdom (53.8%), and those involved in research methods as project or dissertation supervisors for taught Master's degree programmes (47.5%). Since the respondents were principally academics with a documented interest in research methodology and methods, they can be considered to be a purposive sample comprising critical cases. It seems likely that if misconceptions are prevalent with this sample, other academics are also likely to hold them (Patton, 2002).

In the analysis, we generated frequency tables and computed the proportion of respondents that hold the misconception (p) together with the standard error of sample proportion ($SE(p)$). In computing p and $SE(p)$, the 'don't know' responses were not considered to represent misconceptions, but highlight absence of statistical knowledge. To test the null hypothesis that the response (agree, disagree, don't know) was independent of the preferred research method (qualitative, quantitative, mixed methods), the

Chi-squared (χ^2) test was used. Due to the presence of 'cells with expected counts less than 5', the assumptions of the asymptotic method could not be met. So, we used the exact significance since "the exact calculation always produces a reliable result, regardless of size, distribution, sparseness, or balance of data (Mehta & Patel, 2010, p. 3). As a measure of effect size, we used Cramer's *V*.

7 Findings

Table 1 provides a summary of the responses for each of the 30 items addressed in this study. It is clear that statistical misconceptions are pervasive among academics with a special interest in business research methods. In fact, the proportion of respondents that hold particular statistical misconceptions reached a 76.0% (*SE(p)* = 0.05) for the statement '*Statistical indices of reliability and validity document important attributes of an instrument (e.g. test or questionnaire)*'.

Table 1: Academics' mis/conceptions regarding statistical thinking

Survey items pertaining to statistical mis/conceptions	A	D	DK	p SE(p)
Descriptive Statistics				
A concise way of summarising a data set is to use an appropriate measure of central tendency accompanied by a measure of spread (Q11)	52	<u>7</u>	21	0.09 0.03
If a set of scores forms a positively skewed distribution, the mean is greater than the median which is greater than the mode. On the other hand if a distribution of scores is negatively skewed, the mean is less than the median which is less than the mode (Q25)	<u>32</u>	12	36	0.40 0.05
Standard scores such as z-scores are normally distributed (Q2)	<u>35</u>	17	28	0.44 0.06
A single outlier will not greatly influence the value of Pearson's r, especially when N is large (Q26)	<u>33</u>	16	31	0.41 0.05
Correlation never implies causation (Q9)	<u>49</u>	24	7	0.61 0.05

Survey items pertaining to statistical mis/conceptions	A	D	DK	p SE(p)
Design Strategies				
Sampling				
Every sample possesses sampling error provided the population is not totally homogeneous or the sample size is equal to the population size (Q18)	58	<u>11</u>	11	0.14 0.04
A random sample is a miniature replica of the population (Q1)	<u>44</u>	34	2	0.55 0.06
Larger populations call for larger samples sizes and hence the ratio of sample size to population needs to be considered when determining sample size (Q3)	<u>41</u>	35	4	0.51 0.06
A sample of individuals drawn from a finite population deserves to be called a random sample so long as (i) everyone in the population has an equal chance of receiving an invitation to participate in the study and (ii) random replacements are found for any of the initial invitees who decline to be involved (Q14)	<u>56</u>	15	9	0.70 0.05
A large sample does not guarantee validity (Q16)	74	<u>3</u>	3	0.04 0.02
Sample size determines precision not accuracy. The selection process determines accuracy (Q21)	52	<u>12</u>	16	0.15 0.04
Reliability and Validity				
A high value of Cronbach's alpha indicates that a measuring instrument's items are highly interrelated, thus justifying the claim that the instrument is uni-dimensional in what is measures (Q5)	<u>26</u>	15	39	0.33 0.05
Different procedures for estimating inter-rater reliability yield approximately the same reliability coefficients and so it does not make much difference which procedure is used (Q10)	<u>8</u>	32	40	0.10 0.03
Statistical indices of reliability and validity document important attributes of an instrument (e.g. test or question-	<u>61</u>	4	15	0.76 0.05

Survey items pertaining to statistical mis/conceptions	A	D	DK	p SE(p)
naire) (Q27)				
If Pearson's r is used to determine the predictive validity, range restriction will cause r to underestimate the strength of the relationship between the predictor and criterion variables (Q29)	13	4	63	0.16 0.04
Missing Data				
It is important to plan for missing data and to develop strategies to account for them (Q19)	69	10	1	0.13 0.04
Sensitivity analyses are designed to explore a reasonable range of explanations in order to test the robustness of the results (Q30)	43	6	31	0.08 0.03
Statistical Assumptions				
A violation of the statistical assumptions affects the significance level of a test (Q4)	42	18	20	0.23 0.05
Inferential Statistics				
A statistic is an estimate of a true population parameter (Q15)	41	17	21	0.21 0.05
A confidence interval is a statement about the unknown population parameter (Q17)	40	8	32	0.10 0.03
A Type I error (α) represents the probability that one mistakenly rejects a true null hypothesis (i.e. "a false positive") (Q28)	37	7	36	0.09 0.03
Practical significance is focused on the study's possible impact on the work of practitioners or other researchers (Q7)	47	13	20	0.16 0.04
The p-value is the probability that the null hypothesis H_0 is true (Q6)	32	27	21	0.40 0.05
When the whole population is used, no inferential statistics are required since the statistical summary of the data represents a parameter rather than a statistic (Q12)	33	22	25	0.41 0.05
Statistically significant results signify strong relationships between variables or big differences between comparison	42	28	10	0.53 0.06

Survey items pertaining to statistical mis/conceptions <u>groups</u> (Q13)	A	D	DK	p SE(p)
A non-directional alternative hypothe-<u>sis always leads to a two-tailed test whereas a directional alternative hy-pothesis always brings about a one-tailed test</u> (Q24)	<u>28</u>	13	39	0.35 0.05
Regression				
In multiple regression, any statistical relationship between two variables may be altered by additional variables (Q20)	55	<u>15</u>	10	0.19 0.04
<u>When multiple regression is used to predict scores on a criterion variable, the worth of a particular variable is in-dicated by the variable's beta weight (i.e., its standardized beta coefficient)</u> (Q23)	<u>27</u>	6	47	0.34 0.05
<u>In multiple regression, an independent variable that is uncorrelated with the dependent variable ought to be left out of the model because its inclusion won't help to make the coefficient of determination</u> (R^2) <u>larger</u> (Q22)	<u>18</u>	19	43	0.23 0.05
<u>Regression analysis is superior to cor-relational analysis</u> (Q8)	<u>21</u>	48	11	0.26 0.05

Note: A = Agree, D = Disagree, DK = Don't Know, p = pervasiveness of misconception as %, SE (p) = standard error of sample proportion; underlined scores represent faulty thinking; underlined statements represent misconceptions.

In investigating whether the responses varied as a function of the pre-ferred research method of respondents, we found that a significant asso-ciation occurred in only 15 out of the 30 items presented. Three of these statements represented statistical conceptions, namely *'a concise way of summarising a quantitative data set is to use an appropriate measure of central tendency together with a measure of dispersion (spread)'* [$\chi^2(4)$ = 9.97, p = 0.037, V = 0.25], *'the confidence interval is a statement about the unknown parameter'* [$\chi^2(4)$ = 11.11, p = 0.023, V = 0.26] and *'a Type 1 error represents the probability that a a true null hypothesis is rejected (i.e. "a false positive")'* [$\chi^2(4)$ = 25.58, p < 0.001, V = 0.40] . As one would expect, the respondents who prefer quantitative research were the most knowledgeable about these statistical conceptions, followed by those who prefer mixed methods and qualitative methods respectively. The other 11 statements represented statistical misconceptions but here different patterns emerged:

a) For the statement *'different procedures for estimating inter-rater reliability yield approximately the same reliability* coefficients. *Therefore it does not make much difference which procedure is used'* [$\chi^2(4)$ = 15.62, p = 0.003, V = 0.31], respondents who prefer quantitative research were more likely to disagree with this faulty statement; those who prefer qualitative and mixed methods were more likely to admit that they don't know.

b) For the two statements *'larger populations call for larger sample sizes and hence the ratio of sample size to population needs to be considered when determining sample size'* [$\chi^2(4)$ = 9.33, exact sig. = 0.044, V = 0.24] and *'statistically significant results signify strong relationships between variables or big differences between comparison groups'* [$\chi^2(4)$ = 12.79, p = 0.011, V = 0.28], those who prefer qualitative and mixed methods were more likely to hold these misconceptions while quantitative researchers were more likely to disagree.

c) For the statement 'Statistical indices of reliability and validity document important attributes of an instrument (e.g. test or questionnaire' [$\chi^2(4)$ = 10.79, p = 0.024, V = 0.26], those who prefer quantitative research were the most likely to hold this misconception, followed by those who prefer mixed methods and qualitative research respectively.

d) For the remaining eight statements - *'standard scores such as z-scores are normally distributed'* [$\chi^2(4)$ = 20.81, p < 0.001, V = 0.36], *'a high value of Cronbach's alpha indicates that a measuring instrument's items are highly interrelated, thus justifying the claim that the instrument is uni-dimensional in what is measures'* [$\chi^2(4)$ = 20.95, p < 0.001, V = 0.36], *'the p-value is the probability that the null hypothesis H_0 is true* [$\chi^2(4)$ = 18.97, p = 0.001, V = 0.34], *'in multiple regression, an independent variable that is uncorrelated with the dependent variable ought to be left out of the model because its inclusion won't help to make the correlation of determination (R^2) larger'* [$\chi^2(4)$ = 25.69, p < 0.001, V = 0.40], *'when multiple regression is used to predict scores on a criterion variable, the worth of a particular predictor is indicated by the variable's estimated beta weight (i.e. its standardized regression* *coefficient'* [$\chi^2(4)$ = 21.82, p < 0.001, V = 0.37], *'a non-directional alternative hypothesis always leads to a two-tailed test whereas a directional alternative hypothesis always brings about a one-tailed test'* [$\chi^2(4)$ = 17.46, p = 0.001, V = 0.33], *'if a set of scores forms a positively skewed distribution, the mean is greater than the median which is greater than the mode...'* [$\chi^2(4)$ = 27.76, p < 0.001, V = 0.42] and *'a single outlier will not greatly influence the value of Pearson's r, especially when N is large'* [$\chi^2(4)$ = 18.71, p = 0.001, V = 0.34] - the respondents who were most likely to hold the misconceptions were those who prefer quantitative research methods, followed by those who prefer mixed methods and qualitative methods respectively. This unexpected result might be explained by the fact those who prefer qualitative research methods were more likely to admit they 'don't' know', with those who prefer mixed methods doing so at a lesser extent.

8   Discussion
The findings of this study suggest both a lack of knowledge and a high pervasiveness of statistical misconceptions among academics with a special interest in business research methods. However, we do not want to convey the message that the misconceptions we have reported here are pandemic to the field of business and management as that would, unfairly, discredit the work of competent researchers.

When academics cannot separate fact from fiction regarding mainstream statistical concepts, it could be hindering them in making appropriate methodological choices (Good & Hardin, 2009; Huck, 2009; Lance, 2011), not to mention the impact on their student's research efforts (Bezzina & Saunders, 2013). Additionally, academics who are not so conversant with statistical concepts (evidenced by those who opted for "don't know" or withdrew from the survey) might prefer to take a qualitative stance in their research study rather than incorporate in it statistical thinking. The consequence could be that rather than answering the question that they think is the important question, the research question fits the convenient design (Shavelson & Towne, 2004). We believe that this issue warrants attention in the teaching of business research methods.

A second major finding in this study is that in half of statements addressed, the pervasiveness of the misconceptions was not associated with the preferred research method. However, where a significant association was found, in most cases quantitative researchers were more likely to endorse the misconception. This could be attributed to the fact that a number of 'statistical rules of thumb' endorsed by these academics are flawed and, unlike qualitative researchers, they are less likely to be aware of their own lack of knowledge; represented by 'don't know' responses. We hope that this research will help such academics to identify misconceptions and to understand the impact of these on their students. Today, various books and interactive Internet activities are available to help those interested to 'undo' misconceptions, although the strategies suggested for addressing such statistical and methodological misconceptions might themselves require evaluation in future studies.

There are some limitations to our findings that should be noted. First, we used a critical case purposive sample. Consequently it could be argued that this sample is suited more to the logical than the statistical generalisations we have made. Second, the findings of this study are based on a relatively small sample, despite follow-ups to potential respondents restating the web-link and re-emphasizing the deadline. This, combined with the high withdrawal rate might have biased to some extent parameter estimates. Third, the concepts addressed in this study are not exhaustive. Fourth, although we asked respondents to highlight their preferred research method, we believe that the choice of method should be dependent upon the question being answered (Saunders, Lewis & Thornhill, 2012).

9   Concluding comments

The teaching of statistics is often seen as an initiation into rules and procedures which might be seen as attractive and powerful by instructors, yet meaningless by pupils (Bezzina, 2004). Easy practices tend to take the short route by by-passing the detailed study necessary to get it right (Lenth, 2000), As Good and Harding (2009, p. xi) argued, the availability of statistical software packages and high-speed computers "will no more make one a statistician than a scalpel will turn one into a neurosurgeon". Allowing these tools to do our thinking will obscure the true value of statistics when applied correctly in research.

To develop a thorough understanding of the statistical foundations requires careful practice sustained by sound rationale and justification that goes beyond simply applying rules and procedures. To enable this, statistics need to be taught by instructors who, through their expertise are fully aware of and can explain prevalent misconceptions. Where instructors are not statistical experts it is important that, as was the case in for many of our 'qualitative' respondents, as well as at least some of those who withdrew, they recognise their lack of knowledge. We believe that students are more likely to benefit in quantitative research methods classes and courses if they are given the opportunity (i) to get involved in the struggle with the statistical concepts, (ii) to get involved in dialogue and (iii) to focus on formulating reasonable solutions that are timely, accurate, flexible, economical, reliable and easy to understand and use, rather than just applying procedures.

References

Bezzina, F. (2004) "Pupils' Understanding of Probability & Statistics (14-15+): Difficulties and Insights for Instruction", Journal of Maltese Education Research, Vol. 2, No. 1, pp. 53-67.

Bezzina, F. & Saunders, M.N.K. (2013) "The Prevalence of Research Methodology Mis/conceptions among Business and Management Academics", in, Mesquita, A. & Ramos, I. (eds) Proceedings of the 12th European Conference on Research Methodology for Business and Management Studies, Reading, ACPI, pp. 40-47.

Box, G.E.P. & Tiao, G.C. (1964) "A note on criterion robustness and inference robustness", Biometrica, Vol. 51, pp. 169-173.

Brown, D.E. & Clement, J. (1989) "Overcoming misconceptions via analogical reasoning; abstract transfer versus explanatory model construction", Instructional Science, Vol. 18, pp. 237-261.

Bryman, A. (1988) Quality and Quantity in Social Research, Unwin Hyman, London.

Bryman, A. (2012) Social Research Methods (4th edn) Oxford University Press, Oxford.

Bryman, A. & Bell, E. (2011) Business Research Methods (3rd edn), Oxford University Press, Oxford.

Cole, J. C. (2008) "How to deal with missing data", in Osborne, J.W. (ed.), Best practices in quantitative methods, Sage, Thousand Oaks, CA, pp. 214–238.

Cortina, J.M. & Landis, R.S. (2009) "When Small Effect Sizes Tell a Big Story, and When Large Effect Sizes Don't", in Lance C.E. & Vandenberg, R.J. (eds) Statistical and Methodological Myths and Urban Legends, Routledge, London, pp. 287-308.

Eby, L.T., Hurst, C.S. & Butts, M.M. (2009) "Qualitative Research: The Redheaded Stepchild in Organisational and Social Science Research?", in, Lance C.E. & Vandenberg, R.J. (eds) Statistical and Methodological Myths and Urban Legends: Doctrine, Verity and Fable in Organisational and Social Sciences. Routledge, London, pp. 219-246.

Ellis, P.D. (2010) The Essential Guide to Effect Sizes: Statistical power, Meta-Analysis and the interpretation of research results, Cambridge University Press, Cambridge.

Field, A. (2009) Discovering Statistics using SPSS (3rd edn), SAGE, London.

Fisher, R.A. (1922) "On the mathematical foundation of theoertical statistics", Philosophical Transactions of the Royal Society of London. Series A, Containing Papers of a Mathematical or Physical Character, Vol. 222, pp. 309-368.

Garfield, J.B. (1995) "How students learn statistics", International Statistics Review, Vol. 63, pp. 25-34.

Gel, Y., Miao, W. & Gastwirth, J.L. (2005) "The importance of checking the assumptions in underlying statistical analysis: Graphing methods for assessing normality", Jurimetrics, Vol. 46, No. 1, pp. 3-29.

Good, P.I. & Hardin, J.W. (2009) Common Errors in Statistics (and how to avoid them), Wiley, Hoboken, NJ.

Graham, A. (1994) Statistics: An Introduction, Hodder & Stoughton, London.

Hacking, I. (1979) Logic of Statistical inference, Cambridge University Press, Cambridge.

Hair, J.F., Anderson, R.E., Tatham, R.L. & Black. W.C. (1998) Multivariate Data Analysis (5th edn), Prentice Hall, Upper Saddle River, NJ.

Hammersley, M. (1992) "The paradigm wars: Reports from the front." British Journal of Sociology of Education, Vol. 13, No. 1, pp. 131-143.

Hubbard, R. (2004) "Blurring the Distinctions Between p's and a's in Psychological Research", Theory Psychology, Vol. 14, No. 3, pp. 295-327.

Huck, S. W. (2009) Statistical Misconceptions. Psychology Press, London.

Huck, S.W., Cross, T.L. & Clark, S.B. (1986) "Overcoming misconceptions about z-scores", Teaching Statistics, Vol. 8, No. 2, pp. 38-40.

Krzywinski, M. & Altman, N. (2013) "Points of significance: Importance of being uncertain", Nature Methods, Vol. 10, pp. 809-810.

Lance, C.E. (2011), "More Statistical and Methodological Myths and Urban Legends", Organisational Research Methods, Vol.14, No. 2, pp. 279-286.

Lance, C.E. & Vandenberg, R. J. (2009), Statistical and Methodological Myths and Urban Legends: Doctrine, Verity and Fable in Organisational and Social Sciences, Routledge, London.

Lehmann, E.L. & Casella, G. (1998) Theory of Point Estimation (2nd edn), Springer-Verlag, New York.

Lenth, R. V. (2000) Two Sample-Size Practices That I Don't Recommend, available at: http://www.stat.uiowa.edu/~rlenth/Power/2badHabits.pdf (accessed November 28, 2013)

Lincoln, Y. S., & Guba, E. G. (1985) Naturalistic Inquiry, SAGE, Beverly Hills, CA.

Mehta, C.R. & Patel, N.R. (2010) IBM SPSS Exact Tests, SPSS Inc., Cambridge, MA.

Mevareck, Z.R. (1983), "A deep structure model of students' statistical misconceptions", Educational Studies in Mathematics, Vol. 14, pp. 415-429.

Meyers, L.S., Gamst, G. & Guarino, A.J. (2005) Applied multivariate research: Design and interpretation, Sage, Thousand Oaks, CA

Murphy, C.O. & Davidshofer, K.R. (2004) Psychological Testing: Principles and Applications (6th edn), Pearson/Prentice Hall, Upper Saddle River, NJ.

Newman, D.A. (2009) "Missing Data Techniques and Low Response Rates: The Role of Systematic Nonresponse Parameters", in, Lance C.E. & Vandenberg R.J. (eds) Statistical and Methodological Myths and Urban Legends, Routledge, London, pp. 7-36.

Patton, M. (2002) Qualitative Evaluation and Research Methods, SAGE, London.

Saunders, M., Lewis, P. & Thornhill, A. (2012) Research Methods for Business Students (6th edn), Pearson, Harlow.

Robson, C. (2011) Real World Research: A Resource for Users of Social Research Methods in Applied Settings (3rd edn), John Wiley, Chichester.

Seidenfeld, T. (1979) Philosphical Problems of Statistical Inference: Learning from R.A. Fisher, D. Reidel Publ., Dordrecht, Holland.

Shavelson, R.J., & Towne, L. (2004) What drives scientific research in education? Questions, not methods, should drive the enterprise, American Psychological Society Observer, Vol. 17, no. 4, April 2004, [online], http://www.psychologicalscience.org/index.php/uncategorized/what-drives-scientific-research-in-education.html

Smith, J. P., diSessa, A. A. & Roschelle, J. (1993) "Misconceptions Reconceived: A constructivist analysis of knowledge in transition", Journal of the Learning Sciences, Vol. 3, No. 2, pp. 115-163.

Teddlie, C. & Tashakkori, A. (2010) "Overview of contemporary issues in mixed methods research", in Tashakkori, A. & Teddlie, C. (eds), The Sage Handbook of Mixed Methods in Social and Behavioural Research (2nd edn), Sage, Thousand Oaks, CA, pp. 1-41.

Thomas, A.B. (2004) Research Skills for Management Studies, Routledge, London.

Tolmie, A., Muijs, D & McAteer, E. (2011) Quantitative Methods in Education and Social Research using SPSS, Open University Press/McGraw Hill, Maidenhead, Berkshire.

Trochim, W. (2000). The Research Methods Knowledge Base (2nd edn), Atomic Dog Publishing, Cincinnati, OH.

van Belle, G. (2008) Statistical Rules of Thumb (2nd edn), Wiley, Seattle, WA.

von Hippel, P.T. (2005) "Mean, Median and Skew: Correcting a Textbook Rule", Journal of Statistics Education, Vol. 13, No. 2, [online], http://www.amstat.org/publications/jse/v13n2/vonhippel.html

Westen, D. & Rosenthal, R (2003) "Quantifying construct validity: Two simple measures", Journal of Personality and Social Psychology, Vol. 84, No. 3, pp. 608-618.

Combining Focus Groups and Quantitative Research in Organisational Diagnosis

Ellen Martins[1] and Nico Martins[2]
[1]Organisational Diagnostics, Johannesburg, South Africa
[2]Department of Industrial and Organisational Psychology, College of Economic Sciences, Unisa, Pretoria, South Africa

Originally published in ECRM (2014) Conference Proceedings

Editorial Commentary

This study applied the mixed method approach to research by combining focus groups and surveys. The authors' reasoning behind this approach was that it was beneficial in that it provided a better understanding of the problem at hand than if they had used either approach singularly. The study was conducted using employees of a metropolitan corporation. What makes this paper so interesting is the researchers' use of qualitative methodology initially in holding a focus group to develop a survey, using quantitative methodology in analyzing the findings of the survey, and following up with yet another focus group to discuss the employees' opinions of the findings of the survey, adding yet another valuable dimension of mixed method approach. The use of mixed methodology in the study afforded the authors with confidence in their findings and recommendations, as well as ensuring a sense of increased trust and commitment for the employees involved. This study affords an even sounder argument that a mixed research methodology approach is beneficial to gleaning useful information in such an organizational setting.

Abstract: Human resource practitioners and industrial psychologists use focus groups as part of an action research process in their endeavour to improve organisational effectiveness. Action research is a mixture of participation, collaboration and learning by the organisation and the consultant during a process of diagnosis, action planning and implementation. The purpose of the paper is to describe the research methodology that was followed in an organisation in order to explore employee satisfaction levels and inform decision making in improving organisational effectiveness. The diagnostic research process included focus groups as a qualitative method and a survey research process as a quantitative method of research, which can also be classified as a mixed method. The benefit of using a mixed method is that it provides a better understanding of the research problem or issue than either research approach on its own. The benefits and limitations of the survey method and focus groups per se and the benefits of combining the two methods are described, as well as the action research process in relation to the organisational diagnosis research process followed in this research. The research was conducted in a metropolitan organisation with a sample size of 6 715 participants in the survey process. A description of the research methodology is provided, focusing on the purpose, planning, implementation and assessment of the focus groups. The purpose of the research process was clarified with the organisation. A first round of focus groups was conducted in order to adapt/refine the questionnaire. The two focus groups consisted of representatives of all departments and the unions. Open-ended questions were asked to collect qualitative data that would inform the questionnaire, which was then validated through a qualitative laboratory (pre-test). The survey was conducted, the data analysed and the results interpreted. A second round of focus groups was conducted, firstly, giving feedback on the survey results, secondly, verifying the results, and thirdly, exploring the possible causes and solutions to the challenges revealed in the quantitative survey results. Nine focus groups were facilitated with a total of 82 participants. Two initial open-ended questions were asked, followed by probing questions to collect qualitative data, which was then thematically analysed and interpreted. Qualitative data gathered in the two rounds of focus groups was used to inform the interpretations and recommendations in the form of a report and presentation to the management team. This paper provides examples of the findings, proposals of focus group members and recommendations to management. The research methodology followed would be of benefit to any organisation that requires organisational development. A combination of the survey and focus group methodology provided refinement of the questionnaire and a better understanding of the survey results and the organisation. Participation and collaboration of staff members ensured increased commitment, trust and better informed decision making on actions to be implemented to address the challenges the organisation was facing.

Keywords: focus groups, diagnostic process, employee satisfaction, quantitative research, qualitative research, mixed methods

1   Introduction

Organisational leaders regard organisational diagnosis as a key component in the process of improving and developing their organisations to help them gain a competitive advantage (Lee and Brower cited by Martins and Coetzee 2009). Research conducted by Rucci, Kirn and Quinn (1998) indicated that employees' satisfaction levels may have an impact on organisational performance, which may, in turn, influence external customer satisfaction and ultimately financial growth. It is in this context that organisations need to understand how to maintain high employee satisfaction levels and at the same time improve organisational effectiveness. The organisational diagnosis process can be used to uncover employee satisfaction and is often conducted by human resource practitioners and industrial psychologists in collaboration with the organisation as part of an action research process (French and Bell 1999). It is against this backdrop that the researchers in this study developed a combined qualitative and quantitative research approach making use of focus groups and an organisational survey. Combining the quantitative and qualitative research methods can be classified as a mixed method.

The objective of the paper is to describe the research methodology that was followed in an organisation in order to explore employee satisfaction levels and inform decision making in improving organisational effectiveness. The main focus of the paper is on the use of focus groups to gather qualitative data and inform the organisational diagnosis process.

The combination of quantitative and qualitative research as a mixed method, the benefits and limitations of the survey and focus group methodology and the benefits of combining the two methods are discussed, followed by the description of the research methodology.

2   Philosophical stance and strategy of the research enquiry

The research design should be structured in such a way that it enhances the validity of the research findings (Mouton and Marais 1990, Sekaran 1992:92). Cresswell (2003) developed a model that can be used as a guide to develop a research design proposal, which should provide answers to the following three questions that need to be addressed in research design:

155

- What knowledge claims are made by the researcher (positivism, constructivism, advocacy/participatory and/or pragmatism)?
- What strategies of inquiry will inform the procedures (qualitative, quantitative or mixed methods)?
- What methods of data collection and analysis will be used?

The philosophical approach adopted in this research project was a **pragmatism** perspective which was derived from the work of a number of authors cited by Cresswell (2003): Peirce, James, Mead and Dewy (cited by Cherryhomes, 1992) and Rorty (1990), Murphy (1990), Patton (1990) and Cherryholmes (1992). Pragmatism is real-world practice oriented. The research is conducted in a metropolitan organisation. There are many forms of pragmatism with knowledge claims arising "out of situations and consequences rather than antecedent conditions (as in positivism)". The problem instead of the methods is significant. In this research the satisfaction of employees is studied to inform the improvement of organisational effectiveness. Researchers adopt different approaches to understand the problem. Mixed method studies emphasise as a philosophical underpinning the importance of the problem and the use of pluralistic approaches to derive knowledge about the problem (Tashakkori and Teddlie 1998, cited by Cresswell 2003). Pragmatism provides a basis for the knowledge claims that mixed methods draw from both quantitative and qualitative research approaches; researchers have freedom of choice of methods and procedures that best meet their needs and the purpose of the research project; and they use different approaches to collect and analyse data (Cresswell 2003).

The **research strategy of inquiry** that provides direction for procedures (methodologies, Mertens, 1998 cited by Cresswell 2003) in this research design, is the **mixed methods** strategy. According to Cresswell (2003), quantitative methods have been available to the social and human sciences for many years and qualitative methods for the last three or four decades, whereas mixed methods approaches are "new and still developing in form and substance". The emergence of mixed methods as a third methodological movement in the social and behavioural sciences began during the phase of mixed methods as a "movement" during the 1980s (Tashakkori and Teddlie 2003).

The definition of mixed methods research (MMR) or triangulation (Brewerton and Millward 2001) is a contested area, and definitions seem to focus on what is being mixed, different stages in the research process, the extent and purpose of the mixing and what drives the research. When Johnson, Onwuegbuzie and Turner (2007 cited by Cameron, 2011) asked 20 researchers to define MMR, they received 19 different definitions. A simplified definition appeared in the *Journal of Mixed Methods* (2006 cited by Cameron 2011) in its call for papers, namely "research in which the investigator collects, analyses, mixes, and draws inferences from both quantitative and qualitative data in a single study or program of inquiry". The definition that focuses on methodology is deemed sufficient as a description of the methodology followed in this research.

The mixed methods strategy followed in this research was a mix of "sequential procedures" and "concurrent procedures" (Creswell 2003). The research begins with a qualitative method (focus groups) for exploratory purposes and to inform the questionnaire to be used as a quantitative method of data collection, followed by a qualitative method (focus groups) involving detailed exploration of the outcomes of the quantitative method. The concurrent procedure is utilised when both forms of data are integrated in the interpretation of the overall results.

The third question to be answered about the research design is the **specific methods of data collection and analysis** to be utilised. Methods that can be used in mixed methods research range between both open- and closed-ended questions to gather data and focus on numeric versus non-numeric data analysis which includes statistical and text analysis. In this research, the researchers chose the survey method using a questionnaire and focus groups before and after the survey administration process.

In summary, the philosophical stance, strategy of inquiry and methods used in this research as explained above, are depicted in figure 1.

According to Creswell (2003), the researchers who apply mixed methods need to establish a **rationale for why quantitative and qualitative data need to be mixed**. The reasons will become clear in the discussion on the benefits and limitations of the survey and focus group methods.

ELEMENTS OF INQUIRY

* **Alternative Knowledge Claims**

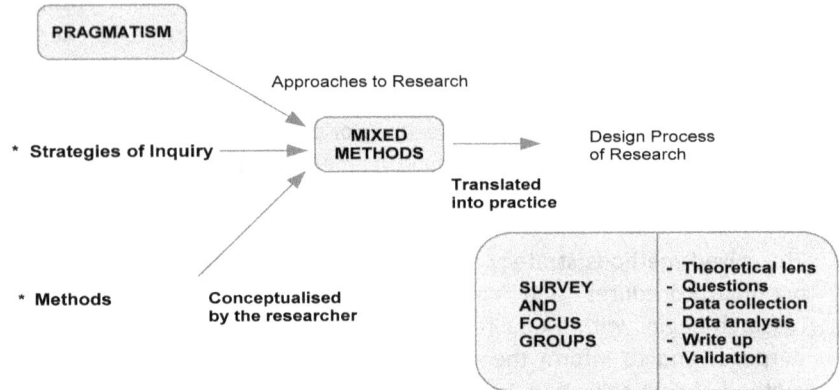

Figure 1: Overview of the research inquiry. Source: Adapted from Creswell (2003)

3 Benefits and limitations of the survey method (quantitative research)

The survey method involves the use of a questionnaire with scale-based questions to gather numerical data.

The following are some of the benefits of the survey method:

- Quantitative research, in particular a survey, produces quantifiable, reliable data that is usually generalisable to a larger population (Anderson and Taylor 2009 cited by Crossman 2013a)
- Quantitative data gathered from the survey method provides vital information for business decisions (Madrigal and McClain 2012).

The following are some of the limitations of the survey method:

- Quantitative research ignores the effects of variables that have not been included in the model and survey instrument because the approach removes the human behaviour from its real-world setting.
- It lacks richness and depth of the data that it presents (Anderson and Taylor 2009 cited by Crossman 2013a)

4 Benefits and limitations of focus groups (qualitative research)

The focus group method enables researchers to gain shared understanding, while individuals are afforded an opportunity to voice their opinions (Tremblay in O'Raghallaigh, Sampson and Murphy 2012 cited by Martins and Martins 2013). The level of interaction and synergy in the group distinguishes focus groups from other approaches (Gibbs; Kritzinger in O'Raghallaigh et al 2012 cited by Martins and Martins 2013). Researchers look for trends in the data rather than performing statistical comparisons (Madrigal and McClain 2013).

The following are some of the benefits of focus groups:
- Flexibility – the researcher can adapt the method as required
- Relatively inexpensive – does not require expensive equipment or extensive research staff (Anderson and Taylor 2009 cited by Crossman 2013b)
- Qualitative data provides details about behaviour, opinions and attitudes that quantitative studies cannot match (Madrigal and McClain 2012)

Focus groups have the following limitations:
- As a qualitative research method on its own it is not appropriate for arriving at statistical descriptions of large populations.
- Reliability may be affected because the information gathered in focus groups is subjective and personal as it is based on the opinions of individuals (Anderson and Taylor 2009 cited by Crossman 2013b).

5 Benefits of combining survey and focus groups methodology

While both quantitative and qualitative research approaches (survey and focus groups) have benefits and limitations, they can be highly effective when combined (Madrigal and McClain 2012).

One of the main benefits of using a multi-method approach in social research is that it gives the researcher greater confidence that the data is valid (Campbell and Fiske 1959, Smith 1975 both cited in Cohen, Manion and Morrison 2007). Validity in this research was obtained by using both a quantitative and a qualitative method. The quantitative data of employees' satisfaction levels was enhanced with the qualitative information gathered in the focus groups. If, for instance, a challenge was exposed by the quantitative data, it was verified and discussed in the second round of focus groups (see phase 3 in figure 2). A single observation provides only a limited view of the complexity of human behaviour and interaction in different situations, with the risk of bias and distortion creeping into the researcher's findings (Cohen et al 2007).

The methods used in tandem in this research to produce full and informative results were based on a combination of the two models of Stekler, McLeroy et al (1992 cited by Nicholls) and are represented as follows in figure 2:

Phase 1: Qualitative method used to develop quantitative measures of instrument (questionnaire)

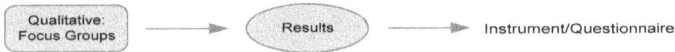

Qualitative: Focus Groups → Results → Instrument/Questionnaire

Phase 2: Quantitative research

Quantitative: Administer Survey → Results

Phase 3: Qualitative method used to explain quantitative findings

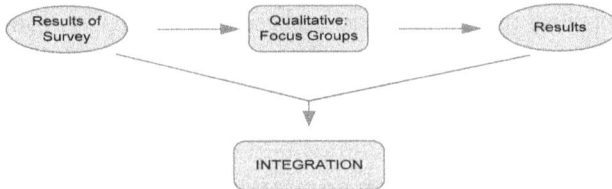

Results of Survey → Qualitative: Focus Groups → Results

INTEGRATION

Figure 2: Model of mixed methods in organisational diagnosis. Source: Adapted from Nichols (2001)

The main focus of this paper is to explain the research methodology that was followed in the organisation and in particular how the focus group method was combined with the survey method. The methodology of focus groups that was followed is briefly discussed in the next section.

6 Research methodology of focus groups

The four phases of focus groups as an academic research method are briefly described below to set the scene for the discussion in paragraph 7 of the research methodology used in the current research (Martins and Martins 2013).

The **problem identification phase** involves the definition of the purpose/goal of the focus groups. The statement of the specific goal becomes the driver of the focus groups and is usually included in a written proposal to obtain buy-in from the management team to conduct the focus groups (Greenbaum 2000). Problem identification is also about generating open-ended questions. Focus groups can be used to test a new concept, develop a questionnaire or questions, generate ideas (Edmunds 1999) or gain a better understanding of the organisation. Questions should be direct, clear, comfortable, brief and asked in a conversational manner (Krueger 1998). The data collected from the questions should be directly related to achieving the purpose of the focus groups (Martins and Martins 2013).

The **planning phase** is about the number of groups, types of people to be invited, group size, location and venue to conduct the focus groups, tools and equipment to be used, time lines for the project and focus group timing (Morgan 1998; Greenbaum 2000). The types of people rely mostly on purposive sampling and consider factors such as job levels, departments and ethnicity in such a way that participants feel free to express their views. Morgan (1998) suggests that smaller groups give each person a chance to talk, but place a burden on each person to carry the conversation, while larger groups might lead to group think. On average, eight to ten participants per group can be used as a guideline. Different tools such as flip charts, pens and post-it notes are useful to capture what people say in focus groups (Anderson and Taylor 2009 cited by Crossman 2013b; Martins and Martins 2013).

The **implementation phase** is about data collection and moderating during the focus groups. According to Krueger (1998), each moderator must bring his or her unique skills and abilities to the moderating experience and treat participants with respect and in a relaxed manner in order to create an atmosphere of willingness to share information. Professional moderators have the advantage that they have experience working with people and keeping the discussion on track. They also create an unbiased and neutral atmosphere. Making use of two moderators is advisable in order to capture as much data as possible because both will be listening and asking questions. The key moderator facilitates the group behaviour, while the assistant moderator takes notes (Krueger 1998).

The **final phase** is the analysis and reporting phase. The collected data has to be retyped, categorised, consolidated and analysed. The focus should be on trends and patterns that reappear among various focus groups (Morgan 1998; Krueger 1998). The report should provide enlightenment by generating knowledge, providing understanding and conveying important, valuable and new information to the organisation/audience (Krueger 1998).

Practical implementation of the research inquiry and the focus groups method is discussed next.

7 Description of research methodology

7.1 Purpose of the research investigation

The purpose of the investigation was to explore employee satisfaction levels and inform decision making in improving organisational effectiveness.

7.2 Overview of the diagnostic research process

The diagnostic research process is a combination of quantitative and qualitative research methods. After clarifying the purpose of the diagnostic project, a round of focus groups was conducted to adapt/refine the questionnaire, followed by a qualitative laboratory study (pre-test) and administration of the survey to collect the quantitative data. The survey results were analysed and interpreted, but to gain further clarity on the data, another round of focus groups was conducted, followed by analysis, interpretation and report writing with recommendations.

The main steps of the process are depicted in figure 3:

The two focus group designs and methodology are discussed below, focusing on the purpose and research questions, planning (research design), implementation (data collection and moderating) and assessment (data analysis and reporting) of the focus groups.

7.3   Focus groups to adapt/refine the questionnaire

The **purpose** of the first round of focus groups was to determine whether the questionnaire would measure all the factors that are required to measure the satisfaction levels of employees. A standard employee satisfaction questionnaire, which had been previously designed and validated, was the base line questionnaire.

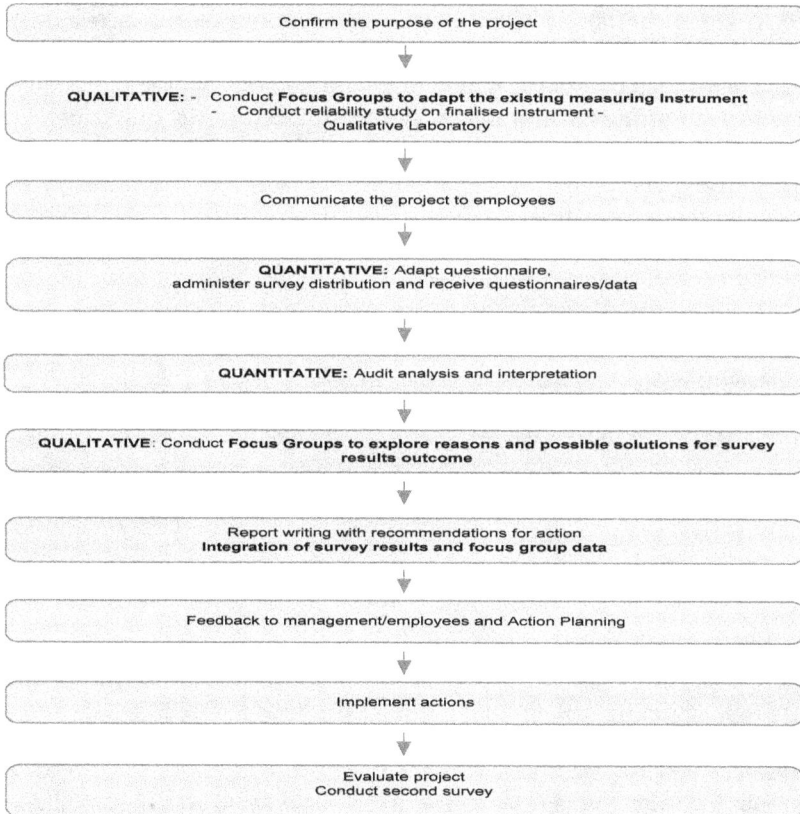

```
┌─────────────────────────────────────────────────────────────┐
│              Confirm the purpose of the project              │
└─────────────────────────────────────────────────────────────┘
                             ↓
┌─────────────────────────────────────────────────────────────┐
│ QUALITATIVE: -  Conduct Focus Groups to adapt the existing    │
│                 measuring Instrument                          │
│              -  Conduct reliability study on finalised         │
│                 instrument -                                  │
│                 Qualitative Laboratory                        │
└─────────────────────────────────────────────────────────────┘
                             ↓
┌─────────────────────────────────────────────────────────────┐
│            Communicate the project to employees              │
└─────────────────────────────────────────────────────────────┘
                             ↓
┌─────────────────────────────────────────────────────────────┐
│         QUANTITATIVE: Adapt questionnaire,                    │
│ administer survey distribution and receive questionnaires/data│
└─────────────────────────────────────────────────────────────┘
                             ↓
┌─────────────────────────────────────────────────────────────┐
│     QUANTITATIVE: Audit analysis and interpretation          │
└─────────────────────────────────────────────────────────────┘
                             ↓
┌─────────────────────────────────────────────────────────────┐
│ QUALITATIVE: Conduct Focus Groups to explore reasons and     │
│              possible solutions for survey results outcome   │
└─────────────────────────────────────────────────────────────┘
                             ↓
┌─────────────────────────────────────────────────────────────┐
│        Report writing with recommendations for action        │
│    Integration of survey results and focus group data        │
└─────────────────────────────────────────────────────────────┘
                             ↓
┌─────────────────────────────────────────────────────────────┐
│  Feedback to management/employees and Action Planning        │
└─────────────────────────────────────────────────────────────┘
                             ↓
┌─────────────────────────────────────────────────────────────┐
│                     Implement actions                        │
└─────────────────────────────────────────────────────────────┘
                             ↓
┌─────────────────────────────────────────────────────────────┐
│                   Evaluate project                           │
│                 Conduct second survey                        │
└─────────────────────────────────────────────────────────────┘
```

Figure 3: Organisational diagnostic process combining quantitative and qualitative methods

Two initial open-ended questions were asked to collect the qualitative data:

*   What do you experience as positive in the organisation?

- If you had the opportunity, what would you change in the organi-sation?

These questions were followed up with more in-depth probing questions as needed. According to Borg and Mastrangelo (2008), workshops (focus groups) afford researchers the opportunity to discuss, clarify and refine all suggestions immediately. In the current study, the data gathered through focus group contributions and discussions indicated themes or elements that needed to be measured and added to the questionnaire. Answers to the open-ended questions pointed to topics/themes. For example: a mem-ber in each of the focus groups raised 'outsourced services as something that they would change in the organisation if they had the opportunity'. The researchers asked the group whether they all agreed that it was a chal-lenge to the organisation. Upon reaching consensus the topic was further discussed.

Typical questions asked, were:

Question: Why is 'outsourced services' a challenge to your organisation?

Answers:
We have lost control over the business.
It takes long to get hold of the service provider.

Question: How does it affect your satisfaction levels?

Answers:
It creates conflict situations between us and the service provider.
We don't know how to solve issues with the service provider?

The fact that the topic of outsourced services was raised in both focus groups indicated to the researchers that it might be an area that should be measured in the questionnaire. Obtaining the quantitative responses of the sample group would then be a way of verifying the information gath-ered in the first round of focus groups. The guidelines that were applied in the focus groups during probing and discussions, were clarifying and sum-marizing, synthesizing and generalizing, probing and questioning, listening and reflecting feelings (Brown, 2011).

The **research design** entailed the compilation of two focus groups comprising representatives of all departments and the unions to gain a broad overview of the positive and challenging aspects of employee satisfaction. A total of 20 people participated in the two focus groups. Making use of only two focus groups and a relatively small number of participants was deemed sufficient since the questionnaire already existed and the purpose of the focus groups was simply to verify the questions and possibly add a number of questions that were specific to the organisation. The duration of each focus group was one and a half hours.

During the **implementation** phase, the focus groups were conducted by two professional moderators with consulting and moderating experience, in order to collect as much data as possible. The discussions were guided by probing questions to further clarify contributions by participants and keep the discussion on track, without leading participants (Greenbaum 2000). The key moderator facilitated group behaviour and the assistant moderator captured the ideas on a flip chart. Both moderators listened and asked questions to ensure that their understanding of the data collected was correct (Krueger 1998).

During the **data analysis** and questionnaire adaption phase, a manual process of thematic content analysis was followed to identify themes in the data. Factual data was separated from non-factual data (which comprises perceptions, skewed facts or interpretations/inferences) (Van Tonder and Dietrichsen 2008 cited by Martins and Martins 2013). The analysis was driven by the need to determine areas of omission in the existing questionnaire and to formulate questions that would measure the concepts arising from the focus groups that were not covered in the questionnaire. An example of a theme, typical issues raised in the focus groups and the question(s) formulated appear in table 1.

Table 1: Example of theme, content and survey question(s) formulated

Theme	Typical issues raised in focus groups (What would you change?)	Survey questions formulated
Outsourced services	Regain control of outsourced business. Not in total control of business – 100% out-sourced. Clarify issues between our departments and the out-sourced services. Uncertainty about the effec-tiveness of the working rela-tionship between our organi-sation and outsourced com-panies.	Q. I am satisfied that in my department we clarify issues we have with the outsourced services. Q. I am satisfied that the outsourced services add value to our organisation's efficiency. Q. To my knowledge our business plan has been clarified with our out-sourced services. Q. I am satisfied with the manner in which we solve issues with our outsourced services

The theme of outsourced services does not usually form part of a typical employee satisfaction survey, but in the organisation in which the diagnosis was conducted, it was an important issue - hence the inclusion of the additional four questions in the questionnaire.

The second phase of this step was to conduct a reliability study by pre-testing the questionnaire. The form of pre-testing used in this project is known as a qualitative laboratory. Methods such as loud thinking, probing or discussion are used to evaluate if all survey items measure what they are supposed to measure (Borg and Mastrangelo 2008). Human resource representatives of all departments participated in this phase. The questionnaire was distributed in a workshop setting. The instructions were to complete the survey and ask questions such as whether the items were clear, each construct was sufficiently covered and the typical rules for item development were adhered to (Borg and Mastrangelo 2008).

7.4   Focus groups to explore and verify the survey results

After the survey had been administered with a sample size of 6 715 respondents in a metropolitan organisation, the quantitative data was analysed and a second round of focus groups conducted. The **purpose** of these focus groups was to give feedback on the survey results, verify the results and explore possible causes and solutions to the challenges that came to light in the quantitative survey results. The groups were asked to confirm the results of the most positive and most challenging outcomes of the survey. They were asked to select an item or items for further exploration and the following two questions were asked:

- Why is it a challenge to the organisation?
- How do you propose the challenge can be addressed in order to improve it?

The first question provided clarity and a better understanding of the survey results. The second question possibly resulted in collaboration and feeling part of the organisation in the sense that employees were afforded the opportunity to express their ideas and opinions.

The **research design** of the second round of focus groups was based on the compilation of nine focus groups with a total of 82 participants. The duration of the sessions was two hours and at least three to five challenges were discussed in each session. Separate focus groups were conducted with the top management team members, the middle management/supervisory levels and lower-level employees so that each group would feel free to participate without fear of victimisation. All races and genders were represented in all of the groups. Two moderators facilitated the focus groups.

A different method of **data collection** was used in the second round of focus groups compared with the first round. Firstly, an overview of the survey results was presented, with a focus on the best and most challenging outcomes of the quantitative analysis. Secondly, participants were informed of the purpose of the focus groups and the ground rules for the session, and the roles of the moderators were explained. Post-it notes and pens were handed out to each member. The first question was asked and members were asked to write down the reasons why they thought the matter being explored was a challenge and possibly provide examples to explain their reasons. The post-it notes were collected, quickly reviewed by the moderators and roughly categorised on the white board/flip chart. The moderator would inform the group of what had been written down. It was then further discussed and clarified, while one moderator added notes on a flip chart. The same process was repeated with the second question.

The methodology that was followed ensured that group think, where the dominant voice in the group might influence others to express themselves in the same way, was controlled by affording each person an opportunity to participate without being influenced by another group member. The methodology also lent itself to more data being collected. It was interesting to note that employees often listed the same information without being influenced by other group members, which was a way of verifying the actual causes of the quantitative research outcomes.

During the **data analysis** phase, all the information collected on the post-it notes was typed for each focus group and then finally integrated into one document. An example of a typical challenge, the reasons for it being a challenge and the possible solutions proposed by the focus group participants are depicted in table 2.

The information collected in the second round of focus groups provided a better understanding of the challenges facing the organisation. Focus group members had the opportunity to express their ideas and opinions creating an atmosphere of collaboration, increased commitment and the expectation that management would act upon the challenges.

Table 2: Challenge, reasons and proposed solutions

Topic: Communication between departments

Developmental aspects	Reasons and examples of why it is an issue/challenge	Proposed solutions
Q43:   There is good communication between departments in our organisation (only 20.1% agreed).

Q42:   My department (where I work) receives information about what is happening in other departments (only 21.3% agreed). | Everyone is focused on their own area – don't care about other departments as long as theirs is good.

Big company – number of departments – not easy to communicate, not necessarily dependent on other departments.

Time pressures and deadlines limit communication with other departments.

Lack of communication causes 1 step forward and 2 steps back. Is a waste of money.

We do not discuss, after a project, what we could improve on in future. | Newsletter to communicate what all departments are doing – brief overview – format: electronic in Excel).

Each department should look inwards on how to improve communication within and if that works, then expand between departments.

Progress meetings to be held once a week.

"Big picture" project information should be communicated in the beginning (specification sign-off).

Introduce kick-off project meetings and retrospective meetings after finalising a project. |

7.5   Report writing and feedback

The information gathered in the focus groups on the challenges facing the organisation was incorporated into the diagnostic report, integrating both quantitative and qualitative research results. Each dimension measured in the survey was discussed in terms of the quantitative outcomes. Qualitative data collected in the first round of focus groups was integrated where applicable with the discussion of the results of the dimensions and statements measured in the survey. The most challenging elements were supported by the information gathered in the second round of focus groups. Based on the inputs on proposed solutions and the knowledge and expertise of the consultants, recommendations to address the challenges and to ensure overall employee satisfaction were included in the report and presented to the top management team.

8   Conclusions

The methods used in tandem in this research produced informative results based on a combination of the two models discussed. The methodology applied ensured that the researchers could report with confidence the survey findings and the recommendations. Importantly, the participation and collaboration of staff members in the focus groups ensured not only increased commitment and trust, but also practical-focused actions to be implemented in order to address the identified challenges. However, as in most surveys, it is imperative that management communicate their intentions and action plan regarding the identified challenges and actions.

References

Borg, I. and Mastrangelo, P. (2008) Employee Surveys in Management: Theories, Tools, and Practical Applications, Hogrefe, Cambridge, MA.

Brewerton, P. and Millward, L. (2001) Organizational Research Methods: A Guide for Students and Researchers, Sage, London.

Brown, D.R. (2011) An Experiential Approach to Organization Development, Pearson, Boston.

Cameron, R. (2011) "Mixed Methods Research: The Five Ps Framework", The Electronic Journal of Business Research Methods, Vol. 9, No. 2, pp 96-108. Available from: www.ejbrm.com. (Accessed 28 December 2013).

Cohen, L. Manion, L. and Morrison, K. (2007) Research Methods in Education, 6th edition, Routledge, London.

Creswell, J.W. (2003) Research Design: Qualitative, Quantitative and Mixed Methods Aproaches, 2nd edition, Sage, Thousand Oaks, CA.

Crossman, A. (2013a) An Overview of Quantitative Research Methods. Available from: http://sociaology.about.com/od/Research/a/Overview-Of-Quantitative-Research-Methods.htm (Accessed 28 December 2013).

Crossman, A. (2013b) An Overview of Qualitative Research Methods. Available from: http://sociaology.about.com/od/Research/a/Overview-Of-Qualitative-Research-Methods.htm. (Accessed 28 December 2013).

Edmunds, H. (1999) The Focus Group Handbook, NTC Business Books, Lincolnwood (Chicago), Illinois.

French, W.L. and Bell, C.H. (1999). Organization Development: Behavioral Science Interventions for Organization Improvement, 6th edition, Prentice-Hall, Upper Saddle River, NJ.

Greenbaum, T.L. (2000) Moderating Focus Groups: A Practical Guide for Group Facilitation, Sage, Thousand Oaks, CA.

Krueger, R.A. (1998) Developing Questions for Focus Groups, (Focus Group Kit 3), Sage, Thousand Oaks, CA.

Madrigal, D. and McClain, B. (2012) Strengths and Weaknesses of Quantitative and Qualitative Research. Available from: http://www.uxmatters.com/mt/archives/2012/09/strengths-and-weaknesses-of-quantitative-and-qualitative-research.php. (Accessed 28 December 2013).

Martins, E.C. and Martins, N. (2013) "Using Focus Groups as a Diagnostic Tool With a Positivistic Approach", in Proceedings of the 12th European Conference on Research Methodology for Business and Management Studies, edited by A. Mesquita and I. Ramos, University of Minho, Guimaraes, Portugal, 4-5 July 2013.

Martins, N. and Coetzee, M. (2009) Applying the Burke-Litwin Model as a Diagnostic Framework for Assessing Organisational Effectiveness, SA Journal of Human Resource Management/SA TydskrifvirMenslikehulpbronbestuur, Vol. 7, No. 1, pp 1-13. Art. #177, 13 pages. DOI: 10.4102/sajhrm.v7i1.177. (Also available at: http://www.sajhrm.co.za.)

Morgan, D.L. (1998) The Focus Group Guidebook, (Focus Group Kit 1), Sage, Thousand Oaks, CA.

Mouton, J. and Marais, H.C. (1990) Basiese Begrippe: Metodologie van die Geesteswetenskappe, Raad vir Geesteswetenskaplike Navorsing, Pretoria.

Nichols, C. (2011) The Advantages of Using Qualitative Research Methods. Available from: http://www.alexander-technique-college.com/files/2011/10/books_articles_qualitative.pdf. (Accessed 28 December 2013)

O'Raghallaigh, P., Sammon, D. and Murphy, C. (2012) "Using Focus Groups to Evaluate Artefacts in Design Research", Proceedings of the 6th European Conference on Information Management and Evaluation, edited by T. Nagle, University of Cork, Ireland, 13-14 September 2012, pp 251-257.

Rucci, A.J., Kern, S.P, and Quin, R.T. (1998) "The Employee-Customer-Profit Chain at Sears", Harvard Business Review, January-February.

Sekaran, U. (1992) Research Methods for Business: A Skill-building Approach, 2nd edition, Wiley, New York, NY.

Tashakkari, A and Teddlie, C. (2003) "The Past and Future of Mixed Methods Research: From Data Triangulation to Mixed Model Designs", in Handbook of Mixed Methods in Social and Behavioural Research, edited by A. Tashakkari and C. Teddlie, Sage, Thousand Oaks, CA.